Cambridge Elements ≡

Elements in Translation and Interpreting
edited by
Kirsten Malmkjær
University of Leicester
Sabine Braun
University of Surrey

TRANSLATION AS EXPERIMENTALISM

Exploring Play in Poetics

Tong King Lee
University of Hong Kong

CAMBRIDGE
UNIVERSITY PRESS

University Printing House, Cambridge CB2 8BS, United Kingdom

One Liberty Plaza, 20th Floor, New York, NY 10006, USA

477 Williamstown Road, Port Melbourne, VIC 3207, Australia

314–321, 3rd Floor, Plot 3, Splendor Forum, Jasola District Centre,
New Delhi – 110025, India

103 Penang Road, #05–06/07, Visioncrest Commercial, Singapore 238467

Cambridge University Press is part of the University of Cambridge.

It furthers the University's mission by disseminating knowledge in the pursuit of
education, learning, and research at the highest international levels of excellence.

www.cambridge.org
Information on this title: www.cambridge.org/9781108932950
DOI: 10.1017/9781108917292

© Tong King Lee 2022

When citing this work, please include a reference to the DOI 10.1017/9781108917292

First published 2022

A catalogue record for this publication is available from the British Library.

ISBN 978-1-108-93295-0 Paperback
ISSN 2633-6480 (online)
ISSN 2633-6472 (print)

Translation as Experimentalism

Exploring Play in Poetics

Elements in Translation and Interpreting

DOI: 10.1017/9781108917292
First published online: July 2022

Tong King Lee
University of Hong Kong

Author for correspondence: Tong King Lee, leetk@hku.hk

Abstract: This Element argues for a perspective on literary translation based around the idea of ludification, using concrete poetry as a test case. Unlike rational-scientific models of translating, ludic translation downplays the linear transmission of meaning from one language into another. It foregrounds instead the open-ended, ergodic nature of translation, where the translator engages with and responds to an original work in an experimental and experiential manner. Focussing on memes rather than signs, ludic translation challenges us to adopt an oblique lens on literary texts and deploy verbal as well as non-verbal resources to add value to an original work. Such an approach is especially amenable to negotiating apparently untranslatable writing like concrete poems across languages, modes, and media. This Element questions assumptions about translatability and opens the discursive space of literary writing to transgressive articulation and multimodal performance. This title is also available as Open Access on Cambridge Core

Keywords: translation, concrete poetry, multimodality, memes, untranslatability

ISBNs: 9781108932950 (PB), 9781108917292 (OC)
ISSNs: 2633-6480 (online), 2633-6472 (print)

Contents

1 Play as Paradigm

This study advances a ludic perspective on translation, using my own engagement with concrete poetry as a test case. In English the word 'ludic', originating in the French *ludique* and the Latin *ludĕre*, has mixed connotations. It denotes 'undirected and spontaneously playful behaviour' (*OED*), with its more archaic cognate 'ludification' describing 'an act of deception or mockery' (Merriam-Webster). But the word also denotes 'serious fun'. According to Merriam-Webster, the word was first coined by psychologists to describe what children do and in that sense was synonymous with 'playing':

> [B]ut the word *ludic* caught on, and it's not all child's play anymore. It can refer to architecture that is playful, narrative that is humorous and even satirical, and literature that is light. Ludic is ultimately from the Latin noun *ludus*, which refers to a whole range of fun things – stage shows, games, sports, even jokes. The more familiar word ludicrous also traces back to the same source.[1]

This study adopts the latter understanding of ludification as a mode of communication underpinned by 'serious fun': play, humour, satire, and a certain lightness. It argues that a ludic conception offers a more radically dynamic imaginary of translation than rational-scientific models, in which translation is generally conceived of as a linear and transparent process leading from a source-language text to a target-language text. Rational-scientific models are instrumentalist in conceiving of translation 'as the reproduction or transfer of an invariant that is contained in or caused by the source text, an invariant form, meaning, or effect' (Venuti 2019: 1). Such models are typical of applied translation theories formulated around an understanding of equivalence.

Notably, Eugene Nida proposed the notion of equivalent effect, which posits that 'the relationship between receptor and message should be substantially the same as that which existed between the original receptors and the message' (Nida 1964: 159). Discourse-based theories are not entirely different in their orientation, save for extending their unit of analysis beyond the sentence level to consider such textual aspects as cohesion and thematic and information sequence (see Baker 2018: chapters 5 & 6). Although the functionalist paradigm, exemplified by Skopos theory and the translational action model (see Nord 2018), does turn toward the reception side of the translation process, it is principally concerned with fulfilling specific commissions imposed on translators rather than, say, facilitating creative or critical work through translation. It is therefore still instrumentalist, though more in the sense of being driven by

---

[1] www.merriam-webster.com/dictionary/ludic.

pragmatic imperatives than in Venuti's sense of reproducing 'invariants' in the source text.

Instrumentalist conceptions of translation are, of course, practically useful for industry-related work and will continue to have an important role in pedagogy and practice. Yet they also limit the potential of translation to dialogically engage with the semiotic possibilities of a work as it traverses languages and even transcends language as such. In Lawrence Venuti's (2019: 5–6) polemical terms, instrumentalism 'constitutes a profoundly metaphysical kind of thinking that has stigmatized translation and prevented even the most sophisticated theorists and practitioners from advancing our knowledge and practice of it'. Venuti thus calls upon us to

> STOP thinking of source texts in terms of translatability and untranslatability and of translation as involving loss or gain; START thinking of translation as an interpretive act that can be performed on any source text.
> (Venuti 2019: 175; original emphasis)

Without invalidating the practical value of instrumentalism, this study showcases the performative, ludic dimension of translation. In this respect, it corroborates Venuti's invitation for us to think of translation as 'an interpretive act that can be performed on any source text', although it does not go so far as to censure the ideas of translatability versus untranslatability or loss versus gain. Nor does it propose that a translation should unconditionally divorce itself from the source text in toto. Rather, it imagines translation as working *alongside* an original work, extrapolating the work in oblique fashion and always maintaining semiotic distance and creative tension with it. Hence, translation is not subservient to a source text in a vertical hierarchy but articulates the latter sideways to develop a more expansive intertextual network – what Patrick O'Neill (2014) would call a 'macrotext'. In so doing, translation becomes a risk-taking venture. Translation needs a wager.

At the heart of my argument is the potential of translation to *transgress* and *transcend* the source text. That is, translation subjects an original work to experimental play replete with contingencies and idiosyncrasies, furnishes it with performative resources for aesthetic expression in excess of the linguistic signs, and extrapolates it toward multiple trajectories and plural media. Ludic translation is therefore diametrically opposed, in strategy and in outlook, to what we may call 'straight translation'. Coming from instrumentalist thinking, straight translation generally operates on the basis of linear, semantic equivalence; it approaches an original work with a keen regard to its formal signs and strives toward a singular, closed-ended product.

If straight translation reinforces the vertical filiations between source and target, author and translator, ludic translation opens up a work to differential pathways or lines of flight (à la Deleuze and Guattari 1987), enabling a work to develop rhizomatically across languages, modes, and media. It subverts the top-down relation between original and translation, renders irrelevant traditional assumptions about fidelity, and challenges outcome-based thinking around the question of untranslatability. Through its playful stance with respect to a source text, a ludic approach unravels the Bakhtinian carnivalesque in translation, 'collapsing hierarchies, travestying sacred truths, deflating exalted doctrines and mischievously inverting high and low' (Eagleton 2019: 156). Ludic trans-lation queers the original.

To move away from normative conceptions of translation as the linear transference of meaning, this study uses experimental texts to open up transla-tion to its aporia. Aporia, from Greek *aporos*, denotes impasse: a site of blocked passages, impeded progress, and arrested movement (Rafael 2016: 12). To encounter aporia in translation means to frustrate or even, as the case may be, terminate the translating act. Yet it also brings into relief textual problems that cannot be readily resolved by means of straight translation, thereby releasing the space to bolder interventions that fall outside the usual translator's toolbox. Experimental writing begets experimental translation.

In the following, I will provide an overview of the concept of play, with an eye on how it is approached from the perspective of translation. I begin by introducing ludification as a phenomenon of culture and ask if there is purchase in advancing a ludic approach to translation. I will then probe the idea of translation-as-play, looking at how ludic translation ties in with prevailing trends in the field that emphasize poststructuralist/postcolonial creativities and criticalities. I will then address the question of intersemioticity, focussing on the experimental and experiential features of translation in relation to multimodal environments, following which we will turn to the concept of memes that underlies my account of ludic translation, drawing on relevant studies on internet memes to offer a semiotic framework for understanding memes in literary translation. The section closes with a summary of the key attributes of ludic translation.

The Ludification of Culture

To speak of ludification is to look upon play as a theoretical construct. Here, play does not denote a frivolous or non-serious disposition in contrast with the ethic of work, as in the expression 'work hard and play hard'. On the contrary, play partakes of work. In its classic definition, play describes 'a free activity standing quite consciously outside "ordinary life" as being "not meant",[2] but at the same time absorbing the player intensely and utterly' (Huizinga 1955[1938]: 13). To engage in play is therefore to adopt a perspective that transcends the structures and routines of ordinary life, to temporarily immerse oneself in time–space configurations outside the mundane realm. It also means to participate in a specific mode of relation with people and objects in the real world (Salovaara & Statler 2019: 152), one that promotes the 'reconstruction and deconstruction of pregiven identities and the construction of new playful identities' (Raessens 2006: 55).

In this view, play is manifest in domains of culture conventionally thought to be unrelated or antithetical to leisure and entertainment. Some examples are as follows.

a. *Service marketing*: where play, in the form of gamification (Deterding et al. 2011; Deterding 2012), occurs as 'a process of enhancing a service with affordances for gameful experiences in order to support users' overall value creation' (Huotari & Hamari 2017).

b. *Organizational management*: where gamification arises within open-ended, non-instrumental conversations 'between and among people and their environment' (Salovaara & Statler 2019: 151).

c. *Game studies*: where computer games most obviously exemplify play, though the concept of games can also be applied to non-digital practices (e.g., sport, children's play) that embody a gamic perspective: 'Anything can be turned into a game (even a game can be turned into another game quite easily) and so the determining factor is not the activity but the way one thinks about it, and how one labels it' (Aarseth 2017: n.p.).

d. *Education*: where teaching and learning are couched in game-like tasks on virtual platforms (Raessens 2014: 94) as exemplified, for instance, by the language learning mobile application Duolingo.

e. *Politics*: where political campaigning adopts a playful stance, gaming elements are inducted into decision-making processes by politicians, and comedians become politicians, possibly bringing over traces of their former public personae (Raessens 2014: 94).

f. *Warfare*: where the military develops game-like simulation programs for training purposes, or where the lay understanding of war is increasingly associated with PlayStation (see Raessens 2014: 94).

---

[2] The phrase 'not meant' was originally rendered as 'not serious' in the English translation of Huizinga's book. According to Raessens (2014: 101n20), 'not serious' is a mistranslation of the Dutch *niet gemeend* as per Huizinga's usage. The translation quoted here is Raessens's (2014: 101) correction.

g. *Mobile communication*: where texting, twittering, or instagramming on mobile platforms and applications exhibits a heteroglossic playfulness through the use of emoticons, abbreviations, and invented spellings (cf. Raessens 2014: 94).

h. *Film*: where the narrative structure of modern cinema takes on gamic elements, while video games are increasingly inflected with a cinematic aesthetic (Larsen 2019).

i. *Literature*: where play is involved in ludic digital literature (Ensslin 2014), but also more generally in ergodic (from Greek *ergon*, 'work', and *odos*, 'path', 'way') literature. Ergodic texts require readers to commit 'non-trivial effort' – any form of reading labour beyond linear eye move-ment and page turning – to traverse the text (Aarseth 1997: 1–2), such as making choices that would take them on different pathways within a narrative.

This non-exhaustive list shows that play has a pervasive presence in our daily lives as both affect and motif, engendering what Raessens (2006, 2014) calls the 'ludification of culture'. It is as if a 'playful specter is haunting the world' (Frissen et al. 2015: 9), such that we might in hermeneutic terms be witnessing a 'gamification of existence' in which play becomes an ontological mode of our experiential world (Salovaara & Statler 2019: 151).

The ludification of culture is perhaps most palpable in the contemporary media, whose programmable and networked affordances have intensified the sense of play in mediated cultural productions. It is on this basis that Raessens (2014) proposes a 'ludic turn' in media theory, where concepts and dichotomies from game and play studies (e.g., playability, gaming apparatus, ludoliteracy) offer a 'new interpretative framework' for media studies; this framework serves to highlight 'the important characteristics of and issues in the field of digital media culture and to prepare the ground for new perspectives and action plans' (110). Within this ludic turn, play figures as a heuristic tool 'to shed new light on contemporary media culture, as a lens that makes it possible to have a look at new objects and study them in a particular way' (96).

Translation-as-Play

The question for us is this: can we similarly develop a ludic perspective in translation theory, one that sheds new light on contemporary translation culture, enabling us to understand new textual and semiotic objects as translations and to study them as such?

If ludification entails creativity, one might say the seeds for such a turn have long been sown, for the idea that translation embodies creative expression is a well-attested one in the research literature. Scholars working within the tradition of descriptive translation studies have made a rigorous case for translation to be recognized for its pivotal role in cultural productions across languages and cultures, maintaining that it should be treated on a par with all literary and aesthetic practices (Perteghella & Loffredo 2006; Bassnett & Bush 2007; Boase-Beier et al. 2018; Bassnett 2019; Malmkjær 2020).

Loosely inspired by poststructuralist and postcolonial scholarship, this line of inquiry is based around the central idea that translations are not derivative copies but original compositions in their own right. It has enlarged the ambit of translation to encompass a cluster of related communicative modalities to which *re-*, *cross-*, *inter-*, or *trans* prefixes are attached. It has also empowered the figure of translators by highlighting their proactive, agentive role 'in shaping texts' and 'contribut[ing] to fundamental changes in diverse cultural systems' (Tymoczko 2014: 189). In more activist contexts, translation involves experimenting with semiotic resources in 'prefigurative' practices of exploring alternative ways to imagine society, or drawing on the classical resources of one's culture to develop a critical, shared, 'aspirational' idiom of the streets that 'embod[ies] a communitarian ethos that is missing from the imported vocabulary' of foreign scholarship (Baker 2020: n.p.).

In this connection, play can serve as a lubricant in negotiating the tensions between original and translation. It proffers a conceptual route out of irreconcilable dualities by opening up to the possibilities of creative and critical intertextualities across languages and cultures. It transcends a zero-sum (all-or-nothing) conception under which the translator is either submissive to or subversive of the original text and its author. Instead, play spotlights the liquidity of the source–target interface, from which translational identity formations are engendered.

One notable attempt to use play as a conceptual handle on translation comes from Vicente Rafael. In examining the politics of the vernacular in postcolonial Philippines, Rafael (2016) stages translation-as-play as a multilingual practice from below against the backdrop of imperial oppression with English as a top-down institutional apparatus. For Rafael, play eschews the simple opposition between hegemonic and subaltern languages by reformulating their polarized relationship 'into a kind of indeterminate, ceaseless displacement and dislocation that prevents any particular power relations from congealing' (197). It is through such reformulation that play transforms normativized identities, thereby gaining its politico-ethical force:

> Play in this way is thus something that is connected to the question of freedom. Why do we play? We play because in some sense play offers *a kind of escape*.

It offers *a kind of release*. It opens up an other world and an other life where nothing is stable, *where no one is permanently on top, no one is permanently at the bottom*, where there is a certain kind of joy not so much in controlling the other as in allowing oneself to open up, to become other. So there is a kind of delight, as much as anxiety, in the loss of identity, or the fluidity of identity.

(Rafael 2016: 197; emphasis added)

In Rafael's case study, play is instigated through the tactical use of Tagalog slang, minted 'from the grammatical weave and jagged shards of vernacular languages, creole Spanish, and American English' (43). This brand of youth language is *aporetic* (from aporia). Rather than a transparent vessel that contains and conveys meaning, aporetic language is 'irreducibly material', allowing its practitioners to 'shake it, lump it together, and roll it out over and over again' (13). It does not entail translation in the conventional sense, for there is often no semantic or etymological relation between vernacular and English words (69). Nor does it instance habitualized codeswitching, since it actively appropriates aural-oral slippages between English and Tagalog into new, contingent morphologies. Rather, the two languages are 'juxtaposed in the mode of call and response: *kiskis* returns as kiss, *gasgas* calls forth gash, *luslus* yields loose, *sispsip* breaks into sip' (69). In circulating these slang words, users of the vernacular 'carnivalize' the relation between imperial and subaltern languages and mobilize translation-as-play by virtue of 'being alert to the materiality of languages, beginning with their sounds' (69). It is in this light that ludic translation can be understood as a mechanism in 'democratizing expression' as part of postcolonial language insurgencies (44).

To be sure, the experimental poetics showcased in my study does not have the political resonance of these Tagalog interventions. Nevertheless, the argument that translation-as-play is a method to democratize expression and level the ground of linguistic transaction, such that 'no one is permanently on top, no one is permanently at the bottom', resonates with how the dyadic relation between source and target, author and translator, can be reconfigured through ludic translation. This is particularly the case with overtly performative modes of translation, where the distance from one language to another is mediated not through relations of semantic equivalence but through relations of semiotic analogy grounded in the materialities of representation. Such a translation involves not so much a point-to-point correspondence in meaning but, to borrow Rafael's terms, the dialogic mobilization of communicative resources from one language to *return, call forth, yield*, or *break into* those from another.

Beyond Words

Translation-as-play can be conceived in terms of slippage between language codes, as in Rafael's Tagalog examples above; it can also engage resources from other modes and media. Research in translation has made substantial inroads in this direction, moving beyond verbal texts into multimodal and transmedial productions, thereby shifting critical attention toward translation as an inter-semiotic experience between and across the domains of text, (moving) image, sound, choreographed action, and sensory experience (Campbell & Vidal 2019).

Media theorists have used translation as a trope to understand semiotic transformations across media. In this usage, the term 'media translation' takes on a different valence than the rendering of media-related texts (e.g., journalistic writing) from one language into another. From a media studies perspective, the term refers to the *intermediation* of texts, which means the transposition of texts from one medium into another,[3] as in the digitization of print literature into an interactive archive (Hayles 2005: 89). Following the McLuhanian maxim that the medium is (at least part of) the message, media translation always results in a different work. In Hayles's (2005: 90) words, a shift in media platform, which has to do with *how* a text signifies, changes the way readers navigate around the text, with direct implications for *what* it signifies.

In this connection, the cybertextual practice of John Cayley demonstrates the dynamic of literary writing in networked and programmable environments, an enterprise further complicated by his invocation of translation as a metadiscursive trope. In a piece titled *translation*,[4] Cayley uses an algorithmic technique called transliteral morphing to enact a visual transitioning between languages on the level of the alphabetic letter. By exploring the analogy 'between the discrete nature of alphabetic languages and the discreteness of binary code' (Hayles 2006: 12), Cayley probes the nature of translation on the level of the grapheme. In visually performing translation as corporeal shifts in 'abstracted underlying structures supporting and articulating the "higher-level" relationships between the texts' (Cayley, cited in Hayles 2006: 12), Cayley artfully deconstructs the idea of translation as a lexico-grammatical and mor-phosyntactic process.

Metadiscursively, Cayley's *translation* thus foregrounds translation of a different order, although translation in the usual sense is still there in the background. Set in transliteral morphing are two sets of text in three languages, namely Walter Benjamin's 'On Language as Such and On the Language of

---

[3] Intermediation is not substantially different from the longer-standing term 'remediation', defined by Bolter and Grusin (1999) as 'the way in which one medium is seen by our culture as reforming or improving upon another' (59), pointing to 'the formal logic by which new media refashion prior media forms' (273). Hayles (2005: 33) prefers 'intermediation' because, for her, *inter-* suggests interactivity between media as well as multiple causalities, whereas *re-* implies having a particular medium as a fixated point of origin.

[4] https://programmatology.shadoof.net/?translation.

Man' and snippets from Marcel Proust's *À la Recherche du Temps Perdu*, in their original languages (respectively German and French) and two other language versions (English and French for Benjamin, German and English for Proust). As a result of the program's algorithmic operations, these texts and languages weave in and out of the screen in constant flux, making the reading process feel 'always a bit foreign, uncertain, and vulnerable' (Raley 2016: 124) – all attributes of ludic representation. What comes up on the reading interface is visually discordant and wholly unpredictable, although users can slightly manipulate the interface by means of particular key combinations; for example, pressing shift-d (or -f, -u, -e) allows the German (or French, romanized Ukrainian, English) text to surface on the screen.[5] This interplay between chance and intervention contributes to the 'algorithmic magic' of Cayley's brand of translation, as realized in 'the fragmented quality of the texts, the limited mechanics, and the nonintuitive relation of cut-up codex to versified lines' (Rayley 2016: 124).

The ludic does not necessarily involve sophisticated media technologies. Drawing on a Gadamerian hermeneutics of play, Salovaara and Statler (2019: 151) maintain that in workplace settings, gamification describes 'much more than just the instrumental masking of work tasks as games'. It refers to 'any organizational situation in which open-ended, non-instrumental "conversations" occur between and among people and their environment'; such conversations comprise a back-and-forth modulation, or 'play movement', defined as 'a constant yet undefined movement that circulates and maintains operations'.

Adapting the idea of play movement to a translation context, we might venture to say that ludification, of which gamification is an instantiation, is any process that involves an open-ended, non-instrumentalist, and dialogic interplay across languages, modes, and media. This conception underlies the AHRC-funded network Experiential Translation: Meaning-Making Across Languages and the Arts, which aims to study translation both intersemiotically and interlingually, with a view to developing 'enhanced literacies capable of fostering individual and community agency and engagement' in an interconnected world. The motif of play is implicit in the network's emphasis on intersemiotic translation as a method 'of creation and communication' as well as 'for learning and teaching, collaboration and participation within multilingual, multicultural and multimodal settings'.[6]

In this scheme, translation is construed in terms of a heterogeneous, affective phenomenology, as the synergistic mobilization of resources from different

---

[5] For a detailed analysis of Cayley's work, see Baynham and Lee (2019), chapter 7.
[6] https://experientialtranslation.net/about-2/network/

languages, modes, and media to orchestrate new aesthetic experiences, high-lighting 'the role of individual imagination and artistic creation in education and arts institutions'. In practice, this can take the form of translating a poem into different language versions – each of which may be multilingually constituted – as well as resemiotizing it in tandem in visual, acousmatic, tactile, or kinetic forms, or any combination thereof.

To experience translation is also to radically experiment with it. Earlier, we mentioned how semiotic experimentation is part of prefigurative expressions of social movement agendas. In literature, an illuminating, if extreme, example is offered by Clive Scott, who adopts an embodied, synaesthetic practice to dramatize the reader-translator's psycho-physiological and multisensory engagement with poetry. Scott's translation philosophy is decidedly anti-interpretative (2012: 11), based on a reading stance that is phenomenological as opposed to hermeneutic:

> A reader might indeed ask what a text means, but it is not the purpose of reading to find that particular answer; the function of reading is to generate a fruitful participation in the text, out of which senses ramify and develop, emerge and drop from view, such that the translation is, by nature, both expanding and self-multiplying. (Scott 2019: 89)

The 'fruitful participation' that phenomenological reading generates is a whole-body experience involving, of course, lexical items and grammatical structures, but also typographic or paralinguistic features like typeface, font size, margin, line spacing, and punctuation. Functioning as an ensemble, these various elements 'activate cross-sensory, psycho-physiological responses prior to con-cept and interpretation' (Scott 2012: 11). With this approach, reading is not about extracting meaning as if it were a readily available essence encapsulated in signs. By the same token, translation is not about linearly transferring any such meaning-essence that originates in a source text and finds a resting place in a target text. Rather, it is an ergodic process that 'deepens the experience of contact [with the source text] by diversifying it, by indicating the ways in which it can further diversify' (Scott 2018: 77). It is a 'creative motion' (Scott 2012: 14) that dwells vertically within the liminal zone of experiential contact between translator and text.

Immanent to Scott's programme is a strong element of ludification, based on a mode of reading generated by 'a play of possibilities and probabilities' (Scott 2012: 46), where uncertainty is introduced into the translation process. Hence, the outcome of a translating act is always in flux, contingent as it is on all the surrounding circumstances, including the availability/accessibility of media resources (e.g., coloured paint; see Clive Scott's translation below) and the translator's psycho-physiological condition at a particular point in time and in the sociocultural habitus in which they are embedded.

On this intersemiotic and embodied construal, translation goes beyond language as such. It performs a synaesthetic morphism, 'a sliding across languages or linguistic material, across the senses, across the participating body, in order to achieve an ever-changing inclusivity, a variational play' (Scott 2019: 89). As an experimental site that registers the 'kinaesthetics of reading' (Scott 2012: 12), namely the translator's perceptual response to the stimulus offered by the source text, translation expands and self-multiplies, opening up to develop 'its own multimedial discursive space' (Scott 2019: 89). In so doing, it places the source text 'at the cutting edge of its own progress through time', imbuing an original work with new potentialities and articulating it toward 'its possible futures, its strategy of textual self-regeneration' (Scott 2012: 4).

Scott's experimental approach manifests in jarring forms, standing in stark contrast with straight translation. Whereas straight translation is based on the hermeneutic decoding and recoding of meaning, that is, on *communication*, experimental translation circumvents meaning, aiming instead at *performance* – 'both performance in the text, and performance of the text' (Scott 2012: 5). Performative translation entails dialogic engagement with the source text through the translator's body, with a view to creating multimodal variations on that text in 'excess of the signifier':

> Performance is not only the assumption of body by the text, and of text by the reading or listening body; it is also the multi-sensory activation of the environment by an acting text and of text by an acting environment. And performance, through its own variations, constantly redisposes the literary, understood as an excess of the signifier (over the signified), itself the product of an expanding textual and extra-textual dynamic generated by the participating reader. (Scott 2019: 99)

Instead of focussing on linguistic signs, Scott's approach gives premium to paralinguistic modalities, such as typography, punctuation, varied spacing (e.g., scriptio continua), diacritical marks, page layout, and bibliographical design. The reading interface is often messy, provocative, and palimpsestic, composed of not just linear configurations of words but also layers of graphic inscriptions, such as doodling (in pen and paint), handwriting, crossing out, overwriting, sketching, and colouring (Scott 2012: 30). There is a flamboyant playfulness to these paralinguistic interventions, which are a form of non-trivial effort (Aarseth 1997) on the translator's part, furnishing the linguistic dimension of the translation with rich multimodal textures.

As an illustration, Figure 1 shows Scott's translation of Charles Baudelaire's 'Bohémiens en voyage' (Gypsies on the road) from *Les Fleurs du Mal*. As the title suggests, Baudelaire's poem has to do with nomadic journeys. Scott first translates the French text into a straight English version,

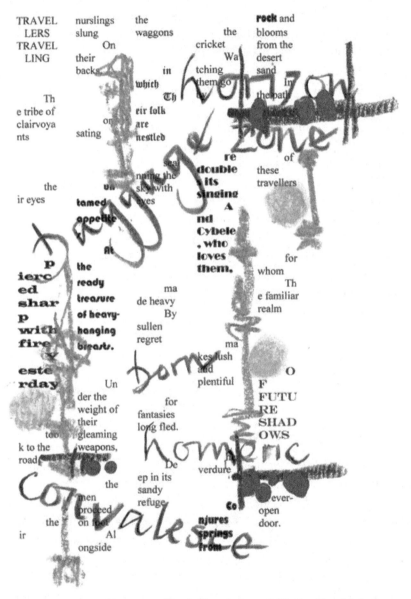

Figure 1 'Travellers Travelling'. Translation of Charles Baudelaire's 'Bohémiens en voyage' by Clive Scott. Reproduced with permission from Clive Scott.

titled 'Travellers Travelling', using it as a backdrop to a multimodal canvas. The first visible shift from the original poem lies in the layout: the translated words are arranged in five columns and segmented at abrupt junctures, creating a vertigo that induces the reader into a 'stuttering, tumbling orientation' (Scott 2019: 101).

Visual modulation is effected through a variation in font type, featuring Wide Latin, Bauhaus 93, Old English Text, Broadway, Gill Sans Ultra Bold, and Engravers MT. Each of these fonts translates a distinct perceptual response or verbal consciousness reflecting the translator's interpretation of the original French wordings. A typographical metaphor for expressing 'a nomadism of utterance', font variation encrypts 'psycho-perceptual shifts and voco-rhythmic modulations' (Scott 2019: 101) in the translator's reading. For instance, a bold typeface may indicate a *forte*; a wider font, a *largo*; and lower case with italic throughout, a *staccato*.

The English translation is then overlaid with scribblings and doodlings in pastels or enamel paint, registering verbal associations triggered by Baudelaire's poetic imagery. Colourings are added, with yellow representing the sun and dark red representing the earth, in line with the nomadic theme. All of these embellishments are meant to convey the poem's environmental ambience, to effectuate 'a cinematic unfolding of days of nomadism through landscapes of changing pigments' (Scott 2019: 101).

Clearly we are looking at a very marked specimen of translation here, one akin to automatic writing in its randomness, chaotic texturing, and non-replicability. Whereas Baudelaire's French poem is a piece of written text, Scott's translation is an artefact created at the intersection of writing and art. The familiar mode of interlingual translation, although present in the form of a fluent English version of Baudelaire, is literally relegated to a back seat on the canvas space. What comes to the fore instead is a multisensory infusion of verbo-graphic expressions, which textualize the translator's subjectivity, 'compels it ... to generate a certain distance from itself, to put itself in the hands of other forces (formal, rhythmic, typographical, etc.)' (Scott 2018: 33). Through its exuberant use of both linguistic and paralinguistic resources, this kind of translation produces an aesthetic remainder (cf. Venuti 2013) by signifying in excess of the source text.[7]

---

[7] Following Lecercle (1990), Venuti (2013: 2) defines remainder in translation as the 'effects that exceed a semantic correspondence according to dictionary definitions and register linguistic and cultural differences in the receiving situation'. For Venuti, all acts of communication release a 'domestic remainder'. This is especially the case with literary translation, where '[t]he source text is rewritten in domestic dialects and discourses, registers and styles, which produce textual effects that signify only in the history of the translating language and culture. The translator may produce these effects to communicate the source text, trying to invent analogues for its forms and themes. But the result will always go beyond any communication to release target-oriented

As compared with straight translation, Scott's experimental translation is open-ended, highly ergodic, and aggressively multimodal. The translator's semiotic input, which crosses the boundary between language and paralanguage, between writing and art, impacts on the translation outcome. Each time the same work is translated, even by the same person, a new piece is born, because the precise combination of resources is contingent on the psychophysiological response of the translator to the work in question at a particular point in time. Translation then becomes a site of potentialities governed as much by chance as by skill. Rather than pointing centripetally toward the source text, translation serves as a prosthetic, directing the source text centrifugally toward its possible, as-yet-unseen shape. A centrifugal translation advocates that

> the text is constantly in search of itself; that it does not comprehend itself; that it has yet to fulfil itself, in paralinguistic realizations, in synaesthetizations; that it does not own its literariness, but that this literariness is unstable, continually re-inventable, always at the text's widening periphery.
>
> (Scott 2011a: 40)

It is easy to see how such a translation praxis can be controversial. Many a reader will find Scott's work untenable and disconcerting, not least because his translations are a genre shock. On the face of the page they are haphazard, such as to be virtually inscrutable to anyone other than the translator himself. Reading appears all but impossible. And if read at all, such translations would generate multiple experiential interpretations depending on the reader's sensory engagement with them, in turn influenced by such factors as the reader's intellectual profile and aesthetic disposition.

Yet I think the beauty of Scott's approach lies precisely in its radical idiosyncrasy in throwing open a ludic and, to my mind, compelling modality of translating poetry. What this mode of translation communicates is the singular experience of embodied reading, which 'capture[s] the individual reading metabolism in all its intricacy, and the perceptually dynamic, multisensory experience we so easily forget that reading is' (Scott 2012: 30). The focal point of such translation practice is therefore not to transfer the meaning of a text as a well-defined essence from one linguistic domain into another – a procedure easily frustrated by experimental forms like concrete poetry, as we will see. It is instead to engender a synaesthetic experience based on a specific, personalized reading of the original text and to perform that experience through the textual body of the translation. This means that, rather than the

---

possibilities of meaning' (Venuti 2013: 14). We may add that concrete poetry demonstrates this point more overtly than any other form of literary writing.

reading of translation with all its assumptions about meaning transfer, we are faced with the *translation of reading* (Scott 2011b).

While I do not go as far as Scott in pursuing a radical visuality in translation, his emphasis on the materialities of language nonetheless informs my own method in translating concrete poetry. In particular, the mobilization of the paralinguistics of writing as affective devices is congenial to my emphasis on semiotic resources rather than linguistic codes in translating experimental texts. It reinforces my proposition that translation is a value-adding intervention that augments a source text through the investment of resources across different repertoires and media. Scott's argument that translation should aim to deepen and diversify one's multisensory contact with a pre-existing work is especially relevant to concrete poetry, a literary form where visual-aural patterning prevails over semantic-hermeneutic meaning.

What is offered here is a conceptual route for us to think away from author-centric, language-based paradigms of translation toward a ludic model in which translation is a multimodal response to a prior work. In practice this means to

> distinguish between a translation which purports, in some form or another, to be 'Baudelaire', and translations which seek, thanks to the continuing activity of the ST [source text], either to co-author with Baudelaire (dialogue/communion), or to produce a not-Baudelaire, where Baudelaire is still present in the 'notness'. (Scott 2012: 3)

The paradoxical turn in the last statement above is pertinent to our ludic ontology of translation. A *not-Baudelaire* translation of Baudelaire is one that fully extrapolates the signifying potential of his work into the semiotic framework of the target language, into the terrain of play. Yet this is not a translator-centric view at the other extreme end of the pole, in which the translator displaces the author as the new Author, a view that banishes the original text while rebranding the translation as a new Original. On the contrary, even if a prior work is translated beyond all recognition, its spectre continues to linger in its new guise as an undercurrent. It is in this sense that Baudelaire can be said to be present, via translation, in his *notness* – an intriguing idea to be taken up again later in relation to the poet whose work I engage with.

Memes and Memesis

To think of translation as play is not tantamount to saying that there are no limits to how one can innovate. Play always presupposes constraints (Raessens 2014: 107) and although literary translation cannot be said to be governed by rule-based gamic systems (Deterding et al. 2011), as in chess or football, the source

text nonetheless serves as a semiotic anchor to restrain an anything-goes attitude. This means, whatever improvisational agency we ascribe to translation,
the bottom line remains that it pivots back to a prior work at the same time as it
draws that work forward, as it were, into a new linguistic or medial space. In
Genette's (1997[1982]: 214) vocabulary for transtextuality, this prior work is
a *hypotext* to which translation is *hypertextually* connected by way of
transposition.

From the perspective of contemporary translation studies, Genette's framework is at once relevant and conservative. Relevant, because it sets out
a spectrum of hypertextual practices, encompassing parody, pastiche, travesty,
caricature, transposition, and forgery, that accounts for how translation is
continuous with other transtextual rewriting practices, such as adaptation,
appropriation, and imitation (Hutcheon 2013; Sanders 2016; Chan 2020).
Conservative, because Genette's view of translation proper is ultimately nega-
tive, attending to how literary texts are 'adversely affected by the inevitable
flaws of translation' (1997[1982]: 215). Corollary to this view is the advice that
the 'wisest thing for the translator would no doubt be to admit that he can only
do badly, and to force himself nevertheless to do as well as he can, which often
means doing *something different*' (217; original emphasis).

Although 'doing something different' does resonate with the construct of
play, we need a performative account operating on a different vocabulary to
positively acknowledge the innovating potential of translation (which Genette
is apparently hesitant to do), though without going to the other extreme of
fetishizing its creative autonomy. Such an account, I suggest, can be grounded
in the concept of *memes*, a term coined by Richard Dawkins in *The Selfish Gene*,
first published in 1976.

Memes are the cultural equivalent of genes; they are units of cultural
transmission that propagate themselves 'by leaping from brain to brain via
a process which, in the broad sense, can be called imitation' (Dawkins 2006:
192). In order for a cultural unit to become a meme, it must be 'sufficiently
distinctive and memorable' (Dawkins 2006: 195), such as to facilitate its
decontextualization from the material or cultural environment in which it
originates and recontextualization in a different material or cultural environment. Memes are everywhere around us, manifesting as ideas (circulating by
word of mouth or other media), images, architectural styles, fashion state-
ments, or popular melodic leitmotifs that can be invoked to conjure up
a particular sensibility.

The proliferation of internet memes with the advent of social media has
brought renewed attention to the theoretical idea of memes. Internet memes,
however, differ from Dawkins's usage in that they are playfully altered by

individuals as they disseminate and develop, whereas Dawkins's memes evolve naturally in accordance with the principles of Darwinian selection. For Dawkins, the usage of the notion of memes by internet aficionados and academics is tantamount to a 'hijacking' of his original term (Solon 2013).

My appropriation of the term, while riffing off Dawkins's, falls more in line with the internet-hijacked version. More specifically in respect of literary translation, I understand memes as the conceptual economy of a work, with the potential in them to be re-entextualized in a different work. Memes embody the abstract aesthetic logic, conceptual motif, or structural principle of a work – its DNA, if you will, to follow through Dawkins's genetic metaphor. They are instantiated in the material signs (words, icons, moving images) we see on a reading or viewing interface (page, screen, stage, installation) and are therefore recoverable on the basis of that final product we see, namely the literary piece. Importantly, memes are mobile; they have the capacity to traverse languages, modes, and media, and in that mobility lies their memic performativity, or *memesis*.

The concept of memesis – compare: *mimesis* – connects closely with how semioticians understand memes in relation to mobile communication. Varis and Blommaert (2015: 36) understand memes as 'multimodal signs in which images and texts are combined'. These signs undergo 'intense resemiotization', a process whereby 'original signs are altered in various ways, generically germane – a kind of "substrate" recognizability would be maintained – but situationally adjusted and altered so as to produce very different communicative effects' (Varis & Blommaert 2015: 36). The iterative production, resemiotization, and dissemination of internet memes are part of a social semiotic practice in which social media users foster membership identities and generate conviviality within virtual communities through phatic acts of communication (such as liking and sharing posts).

For example, 'Keep Calm' (a productive phrase embedded within the template structure 'Keep Calm and XXX') and 'lolspeak' (a pidginized English generated with the 'lolcats' meme) are quintessential internet memes; both are instantiated in varied forms, across diverse discourses and artefacts. They are also ludic: humour is always the point. Varis and Blommaert explain how social media users apply memic resources such as these, while playfully tweaking them to generate manifold versions. These versions are affiliated through their 'memic intertextual recognizability': 'The visual architecture and speech act format of the "original", thus, are the "mobile" elements in memicity here: they provide memic intertextual recognizability, while the textual adjustments redirect the meme towards more specific audiences and reset it in different frames of meaning and use' (Varis & Blommaert 2015: 37).

Therefore, memes do not just replicate, or *mimic*, themselves as they disperse across social media. They are continually adjusted along their trajectory, reoriented 'towards more specific audiences' and re-entextualized 'in different frames of meaning and use', often to ludic effects. At the same time, however, memes also call out to their earlier sources through their intertextual, substrate recognizability, defined as the 'visual architecture and speech act format of the "original"' (Varis & Blommaert 2015: 37).

It is through such interplay between imitation and transformation that memes 'operate via a combination of intertextual, or substrate, recognizability and individual creativity', in which individual users supplement existing memes with an 'accent', with the aim of achieving virality with the accented memes (Varis & Blommaert 2015: 40). In other words, memes perform themselves through a translational dialectic between originating versions and their re-entextualized and resemiotized versions. There is a fractality to this process, as the latter versions themselves can become originals generating further memic (translated) versions. The intertextual or substrate recognizability between memes and their creative variants – their translational relationship – assumes different gradations. These range from a 'purely responsive uptake' ensuing from the 'maximally transparent refocusing of existing memes' (a straight translation, as it were) to an 'active and redirected re-entextualization and resemiotization' (a creative transposition) based on the making of vastly different memes 'less densely connected to existing ones' (Varis & Blommaert 2015: 36, 40).

This semiotic understanding of how internet memes spread virally and generate ludic creativity through re-entextualization and resemiotization fosters my conception of literary memes in translation. As mentioned earlier, literary memes are the abstract and mobile ideas or motifs enregistered in the actual signs deployed in a text. Like social media memes, they can be decontextualized from a prior constellation of signs and then reconstituted in a different constellation of signs. They can also be resemiotized, involving an alteration of their modal properties or media environment, as when a print text is transposed into a digital art installation and imbued with performative elements not available or not utilized in the original. What Varis and Blommaert call intertextual or substrate recognizability can then be understood as degrees of similitude or difference between original and translated memes, where the spectrum from minimal to maximal resemiotization maps loosely onto that from straight translation to creative transposition. I am of course aware that internet memes belong to a different order of things than literary memes, which are the interest of this study. Yet there are grounds to see them as analogically related: from a semiotic perspective, both partake of some form of communication involving the creation, circulation, and consumption of multimodal texts.

What memesis proffers is a method to consider experimental poetry on a different scale level than prototypical approaches to literary translation. To read-and-translate poetry in terms of memes as opposed to signs (words, phrases, expressions) is to circumvent the specificity of linguistic form often fetishized by those who subscribe, sometimes uncritically, to the Frostian cliché 'poetry is what gets lost in translation'. It is to fully acknowledge the potential of translation and translators to innovate, to add value to a piece of literary communication by re-articulating or elaborating upon it in a non-linear, centrifugal fashion. It is also to expand the remit of translation to include versions of a pre-existing work which do not treat its linguistic material directly, or which re-mediate its original form in an entirely different mode and medium, but which nonetheless maintain intertextual recognizability with that work on a substrate, memic level.

In this connection, memesis dovetails with Tymoczko's (2014) account of translation as a cluster concept. The cluster concept enables translation theory to encompass a range of scale levels under its purview, from translations that zoom into specific wordings to those that zoom out to the level of the text as a whole. Memesis operates nearer the latter end of the spectrum, instantiating the frame of transcreation. Although Tymoczko is primarily interested in the categories of representation, transmission, and transculturation, she mentions in a footnote that '[t]he concept transcreation, characteristic of translation in India and also used in Brazilian discourses about translation, might be another productive frame of reference, illuminating many though not all translations' (Tymoczko 2014: 135n31).

Tymoczko's passing mention of transcreation becomes a crucial link for us. Transcreation is intimately associated with the experimental translations of the de Campos brothers – Tymoczko explicitly notes this Brazilian connection (see quotation above) – and with concrete poetry in particular. Sitting at the intersection of translation and writing, transcreation refers to

> a scientific method and philosophy of translation, with attention to the phono-semantic qualities of the text; to the craftsmanship of the artist-creators, who left signs of their personal creativity in each translation, as if it were the signature of an artist on the canvas; and to translation that crosses literatures and languages. (Jackson 2020: 97)

Based on this definition, transcreation, with its attendant emphasis on the performative signatures of translators, is clearly amenable to the idea of translation-as-play. This study rides on Tymoczko's observation that transcreation can serve as a 'productive frame of reference' for illuminating translation and seeks to test her hypothesis on concrete poetry. Using the construct of memes (and memesis), it teases out in empirical detail what happens to an original work within a transcreation frame and theorizes on how a ludic approach to translation can contribute to a nuanced and productive understanding of untranslatability.

Ludic Translation: An Overview

Drawing on the concepts reviewed above, the basic elements of ludic translation may be set out as follows.

a. As a theoretical lens, ludic translation designates a mode of relation between source and target texts: an open-ended, non-instrumental,[8] and dialogic relation in which translation constitutes an experimental and experiential response. Specifically, a pre-existing work provides an initial stimulus to which translation returns, calls forth, yields, and breaks into, and where the translator's sensory proclivities, intellectual aptitude, aesthetic disposition, and even personality are brought to bear on the event. The process is ergodic, entailing non-trivial effort on the translator's part.[9] Any source text presents a translator with potentially different pathways. The pathway taken by the translator is influenced by the material and non-material circumstances surrounding the translating act, including the availability of resources in the target repertoire and their accessibility to the translator at any given point in time-space. Ludic translation is therefore marked by a contingency, where chance and probability play a vital role. There is a vulnerability to it; it is susceptible to failure. Ludic translation entails risk, which must be factored into the economy of translation itself.

b. On the level of practice, ludic translation does not catch on words; it catches on memes, defined as the logical concept or general idea that makes a text 'tick'. A ludic translation approaches an original work obliquely,

---

[8] This is not to say that a ludic lens cannot be applied to translating texts with instrumental value. See Ho (2004) for a case study on translating commercial advertisements based on a value-driven theory and a genetic engineering metaphor. The latter approach is congenial to the idea of memesis (recall that the concept of memes comes from genes), specifically its hypothesis that 'translators retain the "strains" of the source culture, then modify them and implant the modified "genetic material" into the target culture to produce the transgenic text or message' (228).

[9] Non-triviality is to be understood in relative terms and strictly on Aarseth's (1997) definition as any readerly action beyond that of moving one's eyes across the page, flipping pages with one's fingers, or, we might add, simply holding up the book with one's hands. (But handling the book in less conventional ways to access its content would be considered non-trivial; see Lee 2017). It is a commonplace that even translation on a purely linguistic level cannot be considered trivial – as in 'not difficult', although such translations (think legal or administrative translation) do generally progress in linear fashion and require less creative intervention on the translator's part beyond a certain degree of flexibility in lexico-grammatical selection.

transcreating its memes by way of re-entextualization and resemiotization, using discursive, paratextual, and other cognitive-perceptual modalities to enhance the performative value of translation. Ludic translation leverages the slippage within and across languages, modes, and media; it appropriates, accentuates, even invents differences instead of erasing or suppressing them. It represents a productive embrace of uncertainty,[10] creating a semiotic excess or aesthetic remainder through the use of gambits, including on-site improvisation. This means a translation can add value to, and even outperform, a pre-existing work through a tactical investment of multimodal resources found in the target repertoire.

c. In terms of its implication for translation, ludification releases us from the top-down constructs of equivalence and fidelity, facilitating a democratization of expression across languages, modes, and media, while still insisting on a degree of intertextual or substrate recognizability between source and target texts. This gives rise to a new ontology of translation as a centrifugal process that extrapolates an original work toward multiple potential realizations, which together network into a more expansive macrotext. Ludification thus opens up the ambit of translation to draw in new objects of study, such as hyper-performative or digital re-mediations of literary writing. This can drive new pedagogies across the boundary of translation, creative writing, and visual art. It also provides us with a gamic angle on the question of untranslatability, which can be perceived anew as integral to translation: a site of chances and probabilities, trials and errors, rewards and risks, as well as possibilities, including the possibility of failure.

The next section will illustrate these elements at work in the context of concrete poetry in translation.

2 Case Examples: Translating Concrete Poetry

Why concrete poetry? Because it is a limit text, an extreme mode of literary expression that activates the sensory dimensions of language. In the words of the Scottish translator Edwin Morgan, concrete poetry reminds us of 'the literation basis of language and language culture', from which '[p]lay effects readily arise when attention is drawn to rearrangeable components, especially if sound and sight are both involved' (cited in Bassnett 2020: 15). The ludic connection is clear in Morgan's formulation, such that we might think of concrete poetry as 'oblique linguistic games' presenting unique challenges for translation and demanding non-literal solutions (Corbett 2020: 1).

---

[10] I borrow this last phrase from Vidal and Carter (2021, n.p.).

As far as translation is concerned, concrete poetry is aporetic. By virtue of its interest in the subtleties of (semantic) sense, sight, and sound contingent to a particular language, it resists closure on meaning and for this reason is often deemed untranslatable. Therefore, to think of concrete poetry from the perspective of traditional, meaning-based translation theory leads to a foregone conclusion, namely that it is impossible (see Malmkjær 1987: 41).

But this need not be a weakness at all. The formal qualities of concrete poetry that give rise to its apparent untranslatability also make it a good test case for a transgressive, ludic approach to translation. As Bassnett (2020: 19) correctly observes, the object of concrete poetry is 'to startle the reader and to invite that reader to think beyond more traditional boundaries and categories' – and the translator, we may add, is an exemplary reader. More specifically, the inherent playfulness of concrete poetry raises questions about equivalence in translation:

> The playful dimension is also crucial, and here the whole vast area of culture-bound humour also needs to be taken into consideration. What might be more applicable to the translation of concrete poetry therefore is a more functionalist approach, asking what the original is doing and then seeking an equivalent effect. (Bassnett 2020: 19)

Bassnett is right in proposing that translating concrete poetry involves 'asking what the original is doing and then seeking an equivalent effect'. But functionalism, to my mind, is still a restrictive rubric: we should no longer be satisfied with the understanding that translation seeks equivalent effects rather than equivalent meanings, even though the latter is a sound proposition. We need to push further and ask whether translation can add value to a concrete poem by extrapolating its meme obliquely and playfully toward a different language, mode, or medium. In line with that, we need to question prevailing assumptions about untranslatability, including whether we have been invoking it too lightly, as well as too negatively, in the service of linear, meaning-based paradigms of translation.

This section presents illustrations to support my argument, applying the elements of play addressed in the previous section to elucidate a ludic angle on translation. It draws specifically on Chinese concrete poetry, which adds a logographic perspective to the existing literature on concrete poetry in translation, based primarily on alphabetic writing. My source texts come from the award-winning Taiwanese poet Chen Li, who is singular among contemporary Sinophone poets in maintaining a consistent interest in experimental poetry in general and concrete poetry in particular. Chen Li's work has been widely translated and made available in at least eight languages, and the poet himself is a prolific translator who has published the work of such eminent authors as

Pablo Neruda, Jorge Luis Borges, Wisława Szymborska, Sylvia Plath, Octavio Paz, Harold Pinter, and Philip Larkin in Chinese translation. This deep engagement with translation on Chen Li's part, coupled with the fact that he is extremely amenable to having his work transcreated across languages, modes, and media, makes his concrete writing a pivotal case for my investigation.

A Methodological Note

Apart from the first set of examples around the poem 'A War Symphony', I draw on my own English translation of Chen Li's poems to make a case for ludification. Inspired by the work of Clive Scott, I consciously adopt the persona of a ludic translator in practice at the same time as I theorize on my own thinking and output as a researcher. As ludic translation entails brainstorming as part of its trial-and-error process, my translations are a collaborative effort between myself and either a research assistant or a doctoral student. In line with the ludic theme, my co-translators and I imagined ourselves to be playing a semiotic game as a team and trying to 'win' by resolving a concrete poem in the most economical and aesthetically intuitive way.

The aim of my exposition below is to theorize by way of exemplification – that is, to bring the theoretical strands addressed in the previous section in convergence with my own translating experience – and, conversely, to flesh out the empirical details in my application of the idea of translation-as-play to experimental texts. Much of this section is thus written in the style of a praxis account of how I approach concrete poetry as a practitioner, akin to an introspective TAP (think-aloud-protocol) account. Other than the section 'Orchestrating Untranslatability', my translation analysis is largely anecdotal and personal. It foregrounds the specificity and situatedness of the translating act – complete with its whims and bloopers. And although in most cases I do showcase my completed translations, the real analytical interest lies not in the finished products but in the processes, including any stalemates and mishaps, behind their making.

Herein lies the twofold methodological intervention of this study. First, by focussing on the individual translator, I give premium to the singularity and idiosyncrasy of translating. Specifically, in using my own translations as the primary basis for theoretical reflection, I seek to resuscitate the autobiographical dimension in translation. This is meant as a corrective to prevailing methodologies that privilege the general, the objective, and the empirical, hence sidelining the particular, the subjective, and the anecdotal. In a provocative piece on research methods in applied linguistics, Jerry Won Lee maintains that '[t]here is something of a cyclical and self-affirming pattern in applied linguistics research in which assumptions of what counts as knowledge guides methodological considerations, while methodological choices in turn play a role in establishing what counts as knowledge' (Lee 2022). He argues that an alternative methodological and epistemological framework, one that recognizes individualized, idiosyncratic phenomena as legitimate knowledge, is needed to engage with topics 'premised on a disposition that is amenable to "difference," particularly with respect to the potential in that which has been and continues to be neglected or dismissed by dominant research paradigms in applied linguistics' (Lee 2022). The same can be said of the field of translation studies, which has increasingly and extensively looked toward social science as a source of methodologies. A harking back to more intuitive inclinations in humanities research would serve to balance this social-scientific slant.

Second, as mentioned earlier, my focus is on explicating process, even though this usually culminates in some kind of translation product in the end – a virtual reward for playing the translation game, if you will. In my theoretical vision, uncertainty, blockage, failure, and risk are integral rather than inimical to the translating process. They are always already part of the game and need to be fully taken on board in theory rather than treated as undesirables. It is therefore important to regard all the translation outcomes I arrive at as preliminary, contingent, and imperfect. This is meant as a corrective to tendencies in the field to make observations and projections based on neat, final outcomes as opposed to messy and to-and-fro processes.

Orchestrating Untranslatability: 'A War Symphony'

An apt place to begin is Chen Li's highly acclaimed and widely translated poem 'A War Symphony' (Figure 2).[11] The piece has been seen as a classic case of the untranslatable Chinese poem, notably by Chen Li's wife and translator Chang Fen-ling. In her introduction to *The Edge of the Island*, an anthology of Chen's poems in English translation, Chang (2014: 17) justifies her decision to present 'A War Symphony' in its untranslated form:

> Only some of Chen Li's concrete poems are included in this anthology because the linguistic symbolism and cultural specificity of many others defy translation. For example, there is no attempt here to translate the poem 'A War Symphony,' since any relinquishment of its Chinese characters would mean the loss of its poetic charm and the significance of its technical form.

---

[11] All examples of Chen Li's concrete poetry in the original Chinese are found at http://faculty .ndhu.edu.tw/~chenli/visualpoems.htm and reproduced with the poet's permission.

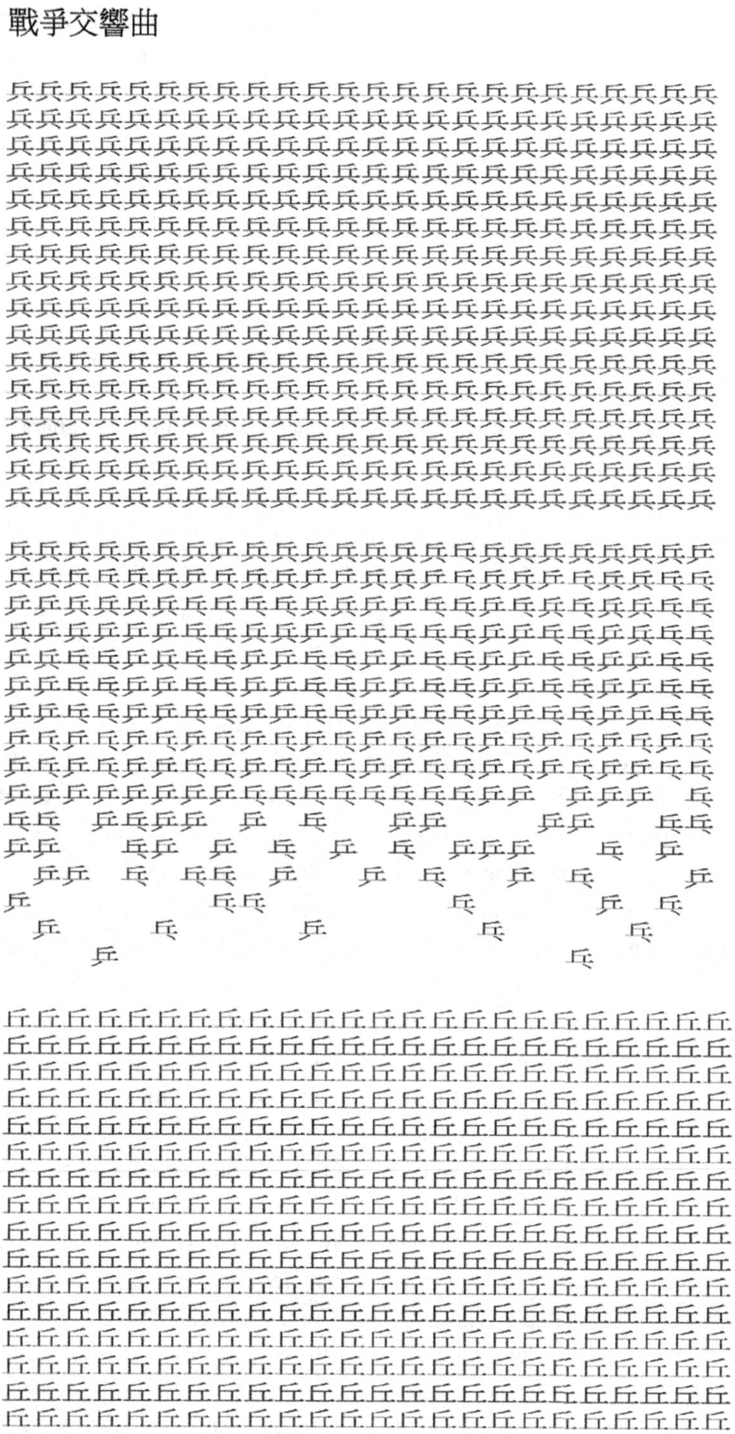

戰爭交響曲

兵兵兵兵兵兵兵兵兵兵兵兵兵兵兵兵兵兵兵兵兵兵兵兵
兵兵兵兵兵兵兵兵兵兵兵兵兵兵兵兵兵兵兵兵兵兵兵兵
兵兵兵兵兵兵兵兵兵兵兵兵兵兵兵兵兵兵兵兵兵兵兵兵
兵兵兵兵兵兵兵兵兵兵兵兵兵兵兵兵兵兵兵兵兵兵兵兵
兵兵兵兵兵兵兵兵兵兵兵兵兵兵兵兵兵兵兵兵兵兵兵兵
兵兵兵兵兵兵兵兵兵兵兵兵兵兵兵兵兵兵兵兵兵兵兵兵
兵兵兵兵兵兵兵兵兵兵兵兵兵兵兵兵兵兵兵兵兵兵兵兵
兵兵兵兵兵兵兵兵兵兵兵兵兵兵兵兵兵兵兵兵兵兵兵兵
兵兵兵兵兵兵兵兵兵兵兵兵兵兵兵兵兵兵兵兵兵兵兵兵
兵兵兵兵兵兵兵兵兵兵兵兵兵兵兵兵兵兵兵兵兵兵兵兵
兵兵兵兵兵兵兵兵兵兵兵兵兵兵兵兵兵兵兵兵兵兵兵兵
兵兵兵兵兵兵兵兵兵兵兵兵兵兵兵兵兵兵兵兵兵兵兵兵
兵兵兵兵兵兵兵兵兵兵兵兵兵兵兵兵兵兵兵兵兵兵兵兵

Figure 2 'A War Symphony'

On one level, one might empathize with Chang's position, for 'A War Symphony' is an extremely cunning poem in its iconic and sonic deployment of Chinese characters. The poem starts with the character 兵 (*bing*), meaning soldier, replicated many times over to represent a troop lined up in neat ranks and files. In a second configuration of characters, we see 兵 interspersed with and transitioning into two onomatopoeic characters: 乒 (*ping*) and 乓 (*pang*). Together the latter two characters form the Chinese word for table tennis – or ping-pong, which derives from the sounds of the Chinese characters. But this semantic sense remains inactive. Instead it is the sound of the characters that are tapped into: in a warring context, *ping* and *pang*, together with *bing,* evoke the plosive sound of gunshots.

There is, further, an etymological sleight of hand in how these two characters are related to the earlier character for soldier. Visually speaking, 乒 and 乓 can be imagined as deriving from 兵 by removing one limb on either side at the bottom of the characters. In the context of the poem, this suggests soldiers being injured, more specifically amputated, in the course of fighting. With this reading, the character 兵 is etymologically refigured, with the two bottom strokes construed as a soldier's legs, when in fact the character is originally an ideograph depicting a hand holding a weapon.

This play with the written script is carried into the final set of characters comprising repetitions of 丘 (*qiu*) which, following the visual economy of the poem, can be interpreted as the character 兵 minus both limbs. This construal, it should be stressed, is not attested in Chinese etymology but is contingent to the structural development of the poem. Yet 丘, like 乒 and 乓, is duplicitous. If 乒 and 乓 are simultaneously onomatopoeic and iconic, then 丘, apart from being a putative truncated version of 兵, is also a full word on its own. It means 'mound' in Chinese and metonymically evokes the image of graves, for traditional Chinese graves are often shaped like mounds and built on elevated ground. In terms of the poem's narrative, the soldiers at the beginning of the text, having gone through brutal bodily contact, eventually die.

Chen Li's war 'symphony' is not merely an aural performance but a complex orchestration of the shape and sound of Chinese characters in tandem; it is the tension and slippage among the sensorial dimensions that account for the poem's aesthetic concept – its meme. Because the poem pivots around the corporeal aspects of these Chinese characters, it is rather convenient to dismiss it as untranslatable. This is the position adopted by Chang Fen-ling, as noted above. A direct fallout of this view is the strategy to *not translate*, which usually means translating the paratexts (mainly the title and original notes, if any) surrounding a poem but not its body text. Hence, Chang's rendition of the above poem translates the original Chinese title; the entire body text of Chinese characters remains intact in the translation.[12] In compensation for the non-translation, Chang supplements a note that summarily explains the relationship among the four characters in the original poem.[13] Translation notes such as this point directly to the perceived untranslatability of the text.

Chang's paratextual resolution belies a conception of translation as a lateral transfer of semantic meaning from one linguistic system to another, a default and perhaps not totally unreasonable understanding when it comes to translating prose and verse. From this perspective, 'A War Symphony' would be considered recalcitrant since either translating or transliterating each of the four characters into English would neutralize the visual-sonic artistry of the original. Yet if we agree that concrete poetry is experimental in its aesthetic, that it is more semiotic than semantic, more about sensuousness than sense (semantic meaning), then surely it is counterproductive to be applying the same criteria as one would in translating normative forms of poetry. Indeed, there is a certain irony in seeking a straight translation of a 'queer', as in formally unconventional, piece like 'A War Symphony'. What is needed instead is a translation that is provocative in its own right, one that performs the original in memesis and not in mimesis.

What concrete poetry does for translation, then, is to call forth a different mode of relation between source and target. In theory, this mode of relation resembles what Philip Lewis calls 'abusive fidelity' with respect to translating Jacques Derrida's writing. Abusive fidelity refers to a translation strategy that 'values experimentation, tampers with usage, seeks to match the polyvalencies and plurivocities or expressive stresses of the original by producing its own' (Lewis 1985: 41). This would seem to fit very well with our ludification agenda for translating concrete poetry. Yet in practice, abusive fidelity is often realized as hyper-literalism. This means closely tracing the form of the source text, in this case Derrida's French, 'trying to reproduce his syntax and lexicon by inventing comparable textual effects – even when they threatened to twist English into strange forms' (Venuti 2003: 253).

Such an intense adherence to form would obviously not work for concrete poetry, whose raison d'être is precisely to resist the linearity and monomodality of reading based on a rule-based decipherment of syntax and lexicon. Concrete poetry is non-linear in constitution and open to multiple pathways of reading. It

---

[12] Apart from Chang's (non-)translation, the poem has been introduced into Dutch, French, Spanish, and Korean using the same method.

[13] The note reads: 'The Chinese character 兵 (pronounced as "bing") means "soldier." 乒 and 乓 (pronounced as "ping" and "pong"), which look like one-legged soldiers, are two onomatopoeic words imitating sounds of collision or gunshots. The character 丘 (pronounced as "chiou") means "hill"' (Chen 2014: 139).

therefore demands a specific mode of reading, which cognitive linguists have glossed as 'skilled linguistic action' (Cowley 2021) and which social semioticians understand as 'a process of design, informed by interest' (Kress & van Leeuwen 2021: 11). This means adopting an 'aesthetic attitude' toward a source text (Malmkjær 2020: 70), although in the case of concrete poems, the focus would be on their multimodal configuration rather than verbal texting. On this view, reading concrete poetry is an 'activity in which wordings play a part', where the wordings are spatially organized into aggregated patternings. The reading interface of concrete poetry is a visual field (see Cowley 2021).

In 'A War Symphony', for instance, the vertical transitioning among the four visually proximate characters (兵, 乒, 乓, 丘) makes up an aggregated patterning that comprises the poem's meme of gradual decomposition, in which soldiers decrescendo their way from life through fighting and into death. To appreciate the poem's narrative and aesthetic, one needs to trace the verbal composition through a visual-aural perspective, as outlined earlier. Reading then becomes writerly, 'quite unlike data processing in that it depends on how readers act to regulate the flow of experience', and how readers act is in turn contingent on 'living bodies that move, look and otherwise enable them to engage with fields of visible patternings' (Cowley 2021).

Now how do we transit from such a mode of reading as skilled action into a mode of ludic translating? Translating linearly on the level of verbal signs would disperse the aggregated patterning of the poem and compromise its meme. The key, then, is to translate one visual-spatial setup into another, that is, to deterritorialize the poem's meme from its aggregated patterning within a particular linguistic constellation and reterritorialize it in a different, but analogical, aggregated patterning within another linguistic constellation. The two patternings, though apparently different, are intertextually related through a substrate, memic recognizability that locates them in a translational relationship. Such a non-linear translation is ergodic; it requires the translator's non-trivial, cognitive-perceptual effort in articulating a new pathway out of the source text beyond its surface-level manifestation.

Let us look at some ludic renditions of 'A War Symphony', which performatively alter the signs in the original Chinese poem in their own different ways while replaying the meme of vertical degradation. The Russian translation, by Papa Huhu, does not translate the full set of Chinese characters in the original but substitutes a set of Russian strings formed around a group of letters in permutation – ВОЙНА (meaning soldier), ВОЙ/ОЙ/НА (mimicking shouts and cries), and НАВОЗ (meaning dung).[14] This combination of signs

---

[14] http://faculty.ndhu.edu.tw/~chenli/Papahuhu.jpg

choreographs the same thematic movement from live to dead soldiers in the original Chinese, while playing on orthographic and phonological resources specific to the Russian language to re-stage the poem's aesthetic motif. A similar strategy is witnessed in an English translation by Bohdan Piasecki. This version starts with repetitions of 'A man', representing (male) soldiers, then morphs into 'Ah-man' and 'Ah-men', with the 'Ah' mimicking the sound of wails, and ends with a series of 'Amen', or prayers for the dead, implying that the men-soldiers have sacrificed themselves.[15]

Each of these translations furnishes auxiliary elements not featured in the original. The Russian version ends with a word meaning 'dung', thus invoking a grimier image of death and hinting more strongly at the undignified nature of war. Piasecki's English version, in turn, ends with a solemn, religious undertone with 'Amen', while its play with 'man'/'men' brings out the gendered dimension of warfare. In their own different ways, the two translations add value to the original Chinese poem in the course of reworking its meme with resources from Russian and English respectively. Instead of smoothing out differences between the source and target systems, they ride on those differences to generate an extensional response to the prior work.

This potential of translation to value-add is vividly illustrated in yet another English translation, by Cosima Bruno (2012: 268), which adopts a Futurist angle in devising a visual-aural solution to the translation problem presented by 'A War Symphony'. Instead of starting with the word for soldier as in the original, this translation starts with repetitions of *tum*, mimicking the sound of marching boots, to metonymically represent the figure of the soldier. In the next turn, *tum* morphs into *bom*, and this is followed by chaotic alternations of several strings permutated around the letters from the two preceding strings – *boum*, *boom*, *toum*, *toumb*, *tuum*, and so forth. Representing artillery and cannon fire, these haphazard onomatopoeic words gradually ease into a monolithic constellation of *tomb*, cohering with the phonic scheme above and, as a bonus, corresponding in meaning with the mound-graves in the final stanza of the original poem.[16]

Bruno's translation is quintessentially ludic. It is an oblique treatment of Chen Li's poem in that it refrains from directly translating the characters (兵, 乒, 乓, 丘). It tackles the Chinese poem as 'a kind of verbal painting', extracting the 'structural elements of repetition, serial development, reversal and mirroring, and precise counts of verbal and typographical or phonic components' (Bruno 2012: 268–9). Using the terms I develop here, the translation goes for

---

[15] http://faculty.ndhu.edu.tw/~chenli/War_BP.jpg
[16] http://faculty.ndhu.edu.tw/~chenli/cosima_s.jpg

the meme, the conceptual schema of the Chinese poem, while manoeuvring around its material signs.

But there is a twist. In the original poem, as we have seen, Chen exploits the architectonics of the Chinese script to enact a gradation across a series of characters by dropping one stroke at a time. The alphabetic script is less amenable to this treatment – one could attempt to reduce the length of alphabetic strings by dropping one letter at a time but that would risk compromising the overall rectangular shape of the poem. Hence, rather than dropping letters, the translation permutates them and in doing so generates even more visual variations than in the original. The translation may not be able to reproduce the same visual deconstruction as the original but through a different aggregated patterning it *exceeds* the original in lexical variety.

The translation does not only go beyond the words in the original; it transcends the verbal dimension of language by recourse to paralinguistics. Typographical and spatial resources are employed to enhance the overall perceptual effect of the poem, such as modulating between upper and lower cases, mixing different fonts and typefaces, and varying the length of the white space between words. Strikingly the poem concludes by gradually shrinking the repetitions of 'tomb' as they run like a vertical scroll until the words (and by extension the soldiers and their sacrifices) become indiscernible – forgotten.

None of the above devices are found in Chen Li's original, inspired as they are by the translator's knowledge of Futurist writing:

> As a process and as a strategy, I do not consider this translation as just a case of 'appropriation'. Rather, it extends beyond literal meaning and mediates between two significantly distant texts (Chen Li's and the Futurist texts), because it aims at supplementing communication through intertextual references and sensorial stimuli. This strategy can perhaps be assimilated to what Haroldo de Campos called 'hypertranslation', in relation to his translation into Portuguese of Cavalcanti 'via Pound via Dante'. (Bruno 2012: 269n29)

This metalinguistic commentary points to the notion of translation as a multimodal *extension* of an original work beyond its semantic meaning and as an intertextual *mediation* between the work and other creative-critical discourses, in this case Futurist writing. This bringing of another practice or discourse to bear on the act of translation recalls what Clive Scott (based on McGann 1990: 28–31) calls 'radial reading'.

Radial reading is a centrifugal and constructivist method of reading that involves 'reading out into, and incorporating, other acts of reading and reference, ancillary texts and contexts, marginal notes, glosses, intertextual materials, such that the constructing of texts is intimately part of an autobiography of reading and associating, a process without end' (Scott 2012: 22). The processual nature of such reading invokes a playful ethic not often associated with poetry translation. Here the source text is seen as

> a nexus of centrifugal forces, generating a series of particular paginal mani-
> festations which collect specific material destinies for themselves across
> time, which undergo changes in their physical constitutions, which multiply
> contexts of operation and thus develop a changeable relation with the literary.
>
> (Scott 2019: 98)

On this view, the motivation of literary translation is to open up a text to an unpredictable network of intertextualities with other practices and discourses, with a view to bringing these extrinsic elements into the reconstitution of the text-in-translation. All of this speaks to the performative agency of translation, which does more than reflect a literary work as manifested in a fixated form. Instead, translation *refracts*, or '[supplements] communication through inter-textual references and sensorial stimuli' (Bruno 2012: 269n29), even *ruptures* a text in order to proliferate its underlying memes centrifugally. The grounds are then set for translation to be seen as a value-adding procedure in literary communication across languages.

These myriad versions of 'A War Symphony' demonstrate the open-endedness of translation which, in principle at least, applies to translating in general, although it comes into sharper relief with limit texts like concrete poetry. Each version of the poem, as we have seen, engages with a different set of semiotic resources to put together a unique constellation of signs to translate the meme, not the words, of the original poem. A sure sign of this is that none of these versions features discursive notes to explain how the original poem works. Each of these versions 'clicks' on its own, and together they accrue into a macro text-complex around the original.

The mode of translating witnessed here is dialogic and ergodic. It is dialogic in that the translation riffs off and responds to the pre-existing work, taking oblique paths to rhizomatically develop the latter's memes into apparently new manifest-ations. Yet it is important to emphasize that the translation maintains intertextual recognizability with the prior text; thus, in 'A War Symphony', all the translations pivot on the same structural movement from one set of signs to another while working around the discrete signs. Without this pivoting, the translations would be disqualified as translations. It is the creative tension between the centrifugal push toward new formations and the centripetal pull toward the source text's meme that defines the dialogic nature of ludic translating.

Ludic translating is also ergodic, for non-trivial effort is always involved. As lexico-grammatical equivalence is downplayed or rendered altogether irrelevant, the solution to the problem presented by the pre-existing work needs to be creatively sought beyond bilingual glossaries, dictionaries, and automated translators. In lieu of words and structures, the ludic translator thinks in terms of mobile resources from linguistic and semiotic repertoires as well as how these resources can be differentially put together, often through trial and error, into economical and aesthetically viable packages. From a ludic perspective, it is thus pertinent to speak of translating as *devising* (solutions to textual problems) or *designing* (new forms for existing motifs).

This line of thinking affords us a different lens on translatability: whether a concrete poem such as 'A War Symphony' is translatable or not is a matter of perspective. If a translator's focus is on rendering written signs and their lexico-grammatical meanings, most concrete poems defy translation except on a facile level, that is, by translating the title, adding an explanatory note, and so forth. If, however, a translator's focus is on performing the concept of an original work with or without rendering the written signs per se, concrete poems are potentially translatable. But that is if we accept a broader rubric of translation that allows it to draw on a full repertoire of resources available in the target context to playfully experiment with a source text – a venture always prone to error and failure.

Such a view of translatability takes chances and exploits the possibility spaces between source and target. It also involves risks and gambits, fully recognizing that any instance of translating could meander several rounds and end up in a cul-de-sac. This could be because the language in which a translator is working does not offer the resources needed to transcreate a particular poem effectively or it could be that those resources are available but the translator has no access to them due to their aptitude, disposition, or temperament.

To my mind, an example of an ineffective translation of 'A War Symphony', apart from Chang's non-translation, is a version by Shen and Wu (2012). This version transposes the orthographic metamorphosis of the original poem into serial mutations of the letter 'i' (representing the self or individuality of soldiers), twisting it out of shape in different directions to signify the loss of limbs and lives. This technique flattens the multimodal ambiguity of the Chinese original; not only is the element of sound erased from the poem (the visual mutations of 'i' are unpronounceable) but the sophisticated sensory landscape in the original is also compromised through the use of a single letter in the alphabet. Chen Li has a similar assessment, maintaining that Shen and Wu's translation 'loses the aspect of musicality, which remains important, even to my visual poetry' (Chen 2020: 62).

The crucial point, however, is not to come up with a set of prescriptive, a priori criteria with which to evaluate the effectiveness of a translation before it even comes into being. The point, rather, is that the possibility of failure is always already integral to ludic translation, which values experimentation; failure is immanent to the game, part of its trials and errors. From this perspective, untranslatability is far from a lamentable condition. It affords a gamic dimension to the translating act, presenting impasses as challenges to be creatively resolved. There are potential rewards to be gained, for instance, a sense of achievement in tackling a difficult poem in a different language, especially if the poem's author is in favour of the translation. Yet like any game player, the translator must also be prepared for a KO, that is, to be knocked out by the source text.

From Pigs to Demons: 'Nation'

I will now proceed to illustrate my own attempts at redesigning Chen Li's concrete poems in English, with an eye on the efficacy of a ludic approach.

Figure 3a shows the poem 'Nation'. Like 'A War Symphony', the piece plays on the iconic materiality of the Chinese script, whereby a character is broken down to its atomic level, on the basis of which a playful, non-etymological reading is derived. The character in question is 家 (*jia*, 'home'), the second morpheme in the Chinese word for nation, 國家 *guojia*, which is the poem's title. The character is deconstructed into two constituent radicals, namely ⼍ (*mi*, 'to cover'), replicated to form the poem's first line, and 豕 (*shi*, 'boar'), multiplied into a rectangular grid.[17] With reference to the title, this spatial deconstruction of a common Chinese character treats the poem's body text as a particular aggregated patterning, giving rise to the ideographic interpretation that a 'nation' is populated by pigs, rather than humans, living under the same metaphorical 'roof'.

As with 'A War Symphony', it is all too easy to pronounce this poem untranslatable from the outset. But as discussed earlier, such a reaction betrays an understanding of translatability in terms of the extent of semantic transferability from one language into another. In attempting to translate this poem into English, zooming in on the semantics ('pigs', 'roof', etc.) would be futile, since English and Chinese have different orthographies and etymologies, thus rendering untranslatability a self-fulfilling proposition. Since a straight translation would inevitably fail us, we might as well enter into ludic mode, which means sidestepping the material signs to capture and respond to the poem's meme.

---

[17] The radical that crowns the character 家 is supposed to be ⼧ (*mian*, 'roof'); etymologically the character means 'pigs under a roof', harking back to ancient societies where animals were reared in houses. The poet was motivated to use ⼍ (without the additional stroke on top) instead of ⼧ by visual factors, namely to create a smooth rectangular shape evoking the angular contours of the key character 國 ('nation'). The additional stroke in ⼧ would have compromised the desired shape (Chen Li, personal communication). Since ⼍ means 'to cover', and is thus semantically coherent with 'roof', the substitution of ⼍ for ⼧ yields a similar visual reading.

國家

Figure 3a Original text of 'Nation'

And what is the meme here? One might phrase it as follows: an ironic subversion of the conventional idea of a nation by way of exposing its unlikely 'occupants'. The phrasing here is deliberately broad-stroke so as to facilitate the meme's pivoting toward a different set of signs; using a narrower construction, for instance by including 'pigs' in the meme's formulation, would limit our options. The question now is which word can serve as the central signifier in the translation as a viable response to the mutated 'home' character in the original, while still keeping the overarching 'nation' theme. This latter theme provides the intertextual, memic recognizability (Varis & Blommaert 2015), which is necessary to justify our intervention as one of translation.

I started brainstorming a list of synonymous English words with my doctoral student (playing the role of co-translator) but to no avail. None of the candidate words derived from a literal translation of the Chinese title – 'nation', 'country', 'state' – makes for meaningful deconstruction such as to produce an aggregated patterning in analogical relation to the one in the original poem. I then decided to contemplate obliquely relevant terms whose dictionary meanings do not correspond to 'nation' but which nonetheless fall within its broad penumbra of associations. In other words, I began to angle on the original text sideways, and this departure from linear thinking opened up new lexical possibilities that would not otherwise have been available to me.

Soon I landed on – and I want to emphasize the chanciness of the word choice here – the term 'democracy'. The latter word describes a political arrangement and is thus thematically resonant with 'nation'. After playing around with the word for a while, I concluded it did not work toward a deconstructive aggregated patterning either. At this juncture, my mind wandered off radially into a different trajectory. At the same time as I was translating 'Nation', I was embarking on a different project in sociolinguistics, and one of my key readings for that project was a paper titled 'New Chinglish and the post-multilingualism challenge' by my friend and mentor Li Wei. That paper was about how Chinese social media users come up with a creative fusion register that corrupts standard English morphology to make a critical point. Among the many New Chinglish examples cited in Li Wei's paper is the portmanteau *democrazy*. *Democrazy* comes from meshing 'democracy' and 'crazy' together into one word. It is used to 'mock the so-called democratic systems of the [W]est and in some parts of Asia where certain legislations such as ownership of firearms can be protected due to political lobbying and, in the case of Taiwan, parliamentarians get into physical fights over disagreement' (Li 2016: 16).

Thinking from New Chinglish back to Chen Li's 'Nation', I pondered using *democrazy* to form the first line of the translated poem, and then using repetitions of 'crazy' to form the rectangular constellation beneath. That might have worked, except that 'crazy' is an adjective; a noun is much preferred to match the figure of speech of 'pig' in the original. It then struck me that, in the spirit of playfulness, I could tweak 'democracy' along New Chinglish lines, using a different inflection than *democrazy*. I looked intently, almost hypnotically, at the string 'demo'. The word 'demon' jumped out at me. Following this intuition, I inserted an 'n' at the midpoint of the word 'democracy' to create a new string.

The result clicked immediately: *demoncracy*. Not only does this invented word visually evoke 'democracy', the embedded noun 'demon' is extractable, just as the 'pig' radical can be singled out from the encompassing 'home'

character in the Chinese poem. As an unexpected remainder, it aurally resonates, in my mind's ear at least, with 'demagoguery', a term often associated with
populist politicians and which etymologically overlaps with 'democracy' (from
the Greek *demos*, 'people'). With these ingredients in place, I was now ready to
respond to the meme in Chen Li's 'Nation' by re-entextualizing it in a different
constellation of signs and to call forth a new aggregated patterning in English to
(out)perform its counterpart in Chinese. Figure 3b shows my rendition.

As we can see, I have kept the overall shape and developmental structure of
the original poem intact. I have not, however, attempted to reproduce the exact
number of repetitions in the body text, which would have bloated my text out of
shape – aesthetics is always a consideration as far as translating concrete poetry

Nation

demoNcracy demoNcracy demoNcracy demoNcracy demoNcracy
demon demon demon demon demon demon demon demon demon
demon demon demon demon demon demon demon demon demon
demon demon demon demon demon demon demon demon demon
demon demon demon demon demon demon demon demon demon
demon demon demon demon demon demon demon demon demon
demon demon demon demon demon demon demon demon demon
demon demon demon demon demon demon demon demon demon
demon demon demon demon demon demon demon demon demon
demon demon demon demon demon demon demon demon demon
demon demon demon demon demon demon demon demon demon
demon demon demon demon demon demon demon demon demon
demon demon demon demon demon demon demon demon demon
demon demon demon demon demon demon demon demon demon
demon demon demon demon demon demon demon demon demon
demon demon demon demon demon demon demon demon demon
demon demon demon demon demon demon demon demon demon
demon demon demon demon demon demon demon demon demon
demon demon demon demon demon demon demon demon demon
demon demon demon demon demon demon demon demon demon
demon demon demon demon demon demon demon demon demon
demon demon demon demon demon demon demon demon demon
demon demon demon demon demon demon demon demon demon
demon demon demon demon demon demon demon demon demon
demon demon demon demon demon demon demon demon demon

Figure 3b English translation of 'Nation'

is concerned. I have translated the original title *guojia* literally as 'Nation' to preserve the crucial irony in the poem. In the first line of the main text, I further made a typographical intervention by capitalizing and bolding the 'n' in *demon-cracy* (hence, demo**N**cracy). This serves to guide readers in segmenting the string in a way that would arrive at the intended reading but also to visually cohere with the 'N' in the titular 'Nation', hence emphasizing the original theme against which the new constellation of signs is to be read.

My approach to translating 'Nation' is distinctively ludic. I sought to creatively respond to the stimulus offered by the material signs in Chen Li's original work, instead of translating those signs on the nose. In the process I allowed myself to read *from the outside in* by incorporating apparently unrelated developments from New Chinglish to formulate a keyword in the translation (compare Bruno's incorporation of Futurist aesthetics into her translation of 'A War Symphony'). It is crucial to acknowledge the serendipities, spontaneities, and subjectivities at work here: it so happened that I was reading about New Chinglish at the point in time, and I decided spontaneously to draw on a potential leitmotif thrown up by the external stimulus, subject to morphological (*democrazy* to *demoncracy*) and typographical (capitalization and bolding) adjustments. Conceivably, if I had been reading something else or been reading nothing at all, I would not have been inspired by the same expression and the outcome of my translation would have been vastly different.

This unpremeditated association with linguistic resources external to the poem speaks to the precept of radial reading, as explained above, namely that 'texts exist in ungovernable strings and clumps, and activate all kinds of achronological relationships' (Scott 2012: 22). Such ungovernable, achronological triggers partake of the ergodicity of ludic translation. Because they originate in extrinsic sources, these triggers are incidental, not immanent, to a work. They yield various possible angles from which a translator can enter a text from outside its box, as it were; each of these angles reveals a potential aspect of the work that may be realized through translation, while downplaying other possible dimensions. Together they give us a holistic grasp of a work in its potential and actual manifestations across languages. And some angles, when attempted in translation, may very well end up in a dead-end, deriving no aesthetically viable solution. Translating ludically entails both rewards and risks.

My English rendition of 'Nation' is the outcome of adopting one such angle based on the circumstances surrounding the translating act, including my own reading experience. The translation does not leech on the Chinese text but adds value to it by offering a unique development of the same meme. Chen Li's poem illustrates, with a touch of cynical humour, that what we call nations are populated by pigs living under several roofs (body politic), perhaps pointing to the laziness or stupidity of the bureaucrats and technocrats running any given country. My English translation, on the other hand, takes a darker turn by revealing more sinister entities dwelling within ostensible democracies or, better still, *demoncracies*.

Capturing Light in Motion: 'White'

The ergodicity of ludic translation comes into sharper relief in my next set of examples, where one source text calls forth several instantiations. In the poem 'White' (Figure 4a), Chen Li stages a pseudo-etymological performance in Chinese similar to that in 'A War Symphony'. The first set of characters features six rows of 白 (*bai*, 'white'), which then degenerate into another six rows of 日 (*ri*, 'sun' or 'day'). The logic of this transition is orthographic: the first character has an additional stroke on the top-left that is 'dropped' to form the second character. Together the two characters form the compound word *bairi*, literally 'white sun', meaning daytime; therefore, the shift from one set of characters to the other implies the movement of the sun's rays or the passage of daytime.

Next in sequence are five rows of 凵 (*kan*, 'dented opening'), formed by deleting two horizontal strokes from the preceding character 日. This is a pictograph that traces the image of a topographical dent, such as a mountain valley. Combined with the first two characters, what we have is an idea of the setting sun bending its rays on earth. This interpretation is sustained in the next sequence, where 凵 is further reduced to a horizontal stroke by dropping the vertical strokes on the two lateral sides – the sun now falls on the horizon. Following four rows of these strokes conjoining into a straight line, the poem ends with several rows of dots, first darker (three rows), then fainter (two rows), and then fainter still (the last row). We might imagine these as dust particles reflecting the vestiges of light, before fading into barely visible particle dots. The sun's setting is now complete.

As with 'A War Symphony', the translation of 'White' as it appears in *The Edge of the Island* leaves the body text alone; only the title is translated (Chen 2014: 197). As I have maintained above, this strategy speaks to a frame of straight translation based on semantic equivalence. The ludic perspective I advocate, in contrast, speaks to a frame of transcreation, which aims to shed a different light on the question of translatability by eliding the semantic and highlighting the semiotic. Rather than treat each individual sign in the Chinese poem carefully as if they were sacrosanct, we look at the text as a visual gestalt. This reading is substantiated by Chen Li's own remark that 'White' recalls in his mind's eye the paintings of Mark Rothko, characterized by the juxtaposition of coloured blocks (Chen 2020: 64).[18] This gives us a clue

---

[18] As Chen Li made this observation as a retroactive reflection on his own work, it is unclear if Mark Rothko's signature visuals had an influence on the spatial patterning in 'White'. For Chen,

Figure 4a Original text of 'White'

as to the meme of the poem, which we might formulate as 'a movement across different intensities of illumination'.

---

the Rothko connection in his work is 'accidental or unconscious' (Chen 2020: 64). Notwithstanding that, it is tempting to see the gradation of colours characteristic of Rothko's art as a visual meme that is resemiotized in Chen's poem.

It is obvious at this point that a straight translation would not do; the question now is how we might translate otherwise. Starting with the word 'White' would take us nowhere, though we nonetheless want to keep the 'moving light' meme so as to maintain the translation's substrate recognizability (Varis & Blommaert 2015) with the original text. With this meme in mind, I began brainstorming keyword ideas, this time with my research assistant. We ran through a list of English words affiliated to, though not necessarily synonymous with, 'light' or 'sun', with an eye to their potential to be contracted into shorter sequences or embedded within longer sequences.

Our strategy here is thus one of attrition, whereby alphabetic strings are reduced in gradations by dropping letters, in analogical translation of how the Chinese characters in the original poem morph into other characters by losing their strokes. Contrast this with Bruno's version of 'A War Symphony' (discussed earlier), which permutates letters within alphabetic strings. Permutation does not work for 'White' because, unlike 'A War Symphony' where sound effects are a central element, 'White' is exclusively visual. The downside to my strategy is that the rectangular shape of the original poem needs to be compromised. That is the 'risk' I resolved to take for want of a better solution.

We failed on several counts; as mentioned earlier, this kind of trial and error is already factored into a gamic view of translation. Then my assistant recalled seeing those mystical photographs of faint white light around one's head. That gave us the keyword 'aura', around which we decided we could work the translation. At this point 'aural' popped up intuitively as a word that could embed 'aura'. This idea was quickly abandoned as it soon became clear that 'aural' diverged from the visual theme of the poem, although it could also provide an interesting counterpoint by resemiotising the visual theme into an aural one.

Keeping my mind's eye on visuality, I then conjured up the image of the polar lights (recalling a documentary I had watched on the Northern Lights in Iceland), that luminous spectacle of coloured lights that can be observed from the Arctic. Happily, we found that the term for this natural phenomenon is 'aurora', which felicitously encapsulates 'aura' within its spelling, though not in its exact form. A brief search on Google brings yet more good news: 'aurora' is Latin for 'dawn' and the name of the goddess of dawn in Roman mythology. These etymologies, hitherto unknown to us, connect with the 日 ('sun', 'day') character in the Chinese poem, again testifying to how serendipity participates in the translator's creative thinking process.

So now we have 'aura' and 'aurora'. The latter string, which is the longer one, needs to come up at the top to preserve the integrity of the poem's meme of visual disintegration. Following the developmental schema of the original poem, that is, the number of rows of the corresponding character blocks in the source text, we set out six rows of 'aurora' followed by six rows of 'aura'. The number of columns, however, is varied, as using the same number of repetitions here as the original would make the translation appear cramped. In ludic translating, the aesthetic may reign over the semantic.

At this point we encountered a bottleneck. 'Aura' cannot be further broken down into a shorter meaningful string with a light or sun theme. We decided to catch on the letter 'u' in 'aura'. This is based on the visual attribute of 'u', the shape of which is similar to that of 凵 in the Chinese poem. There is furthermore a parallel in terms of how the two texts pivot from one orthographic scale to another: just as the Chinese poem goes from full character to radical (the semantic portion of the character), so the English poem goes from word to letter. We aligned five rows of 'u' with the position of 'u' in 'aura' to create the reductive visual; to follow through the diminutive effect, we further reduced 'u' to the shape of an eyelid, which can be construed as a variation on the horizontal stroke in the source text.

Our translation is now shaping up more like a funnel than a rectangle. This is due to the orthographic differences between the two scripts: the architectonic structure of the Chinese character allows it to be deconstructed within a squarish grid; alphabetic strings, however, need to be shortened if we adopt the strategy of letter-attrition (compare: my translation in Figure 4e). We are thus altering the formal contours of Chen Li's poem following the affordances of alphabetic resources. As mentioned earlier, this is a risk-taking procedure, as we are taking liberties with the shape of the concrete poem. But such risk-taking shifts also exemplify the ethos of transcreation. The point, however, is that once this new shape is set down, its integrity needs to be protected in a principled way. For instance, in an early draft we experimented with moving the last several rows of dots in Figure 4a en bloc to the translation and realized this compromised its funnel shape. To keep to the latter shape, we streamlined the dots to ensure they fell in line with the visual development and formal integrity of the transcreated text, while at the same time attending to how the black dots become fainter down the rows until they fade off.

Figure 4b shows one of my translations, retitled 'Aurora'. This retitling is necessary because the original title, 'White', which derives from the first block of characters, is no longer feasible as it does not figure in the translation. The change in title is symptomatic of the transcreative process, signalling that the translation has taken on a divergent trajectory in developing the original meme. This affords contingency to the translating act, whose pathway is influenced by both textual and extra-textual factors, including, as we related above, sudden triggers by incidental thoughts or random associations with other discourses not directly issuing from the task at hand. In translating concrete poetry one needs to

Aurora

aurora aurora aurora aurora aurora aurora aurora aurora aurora aurora
aurora aurora aurora aurora aurora aurora aurora aurora aurora aurora
aurora aurora aurora aurora aurora aurora aurora aurora aurora aurora
aurora aurora aurora aurora aurora aurora aurora aurora aurora aurora
aurora aurora aurora aurora aurora aurora aurora aurora aurora aurora
aurora aurora aurora aurora aurora aurora aurora aurora aurora aurora
a u r a a u r a a u r a a u r a a u r a a u r a a u r a a u r a a u r a a u r a
a u r a a u r a a u r a a u r a a u r a a u r a a u r a a u r a a u r a a u r a
a u r a a u r a a u r a a u r a a u r a a u r a a u r a a u r a a u r a a u r a
a u r a a u r a a u r a a u r a a u r a a u r a a u r a a u r a a u r a a u r a
a u r a a u r a a u r a a u r a a u r a a u r a a u r a a u r a a u r a a u r a
a u r a a u r a a u r a a u r a a u r a a u r a a u r a a u r a a u r a a u r a

u   u   u   u   u   u   u   u   u   u
u   u   u   u   u   u   u   u   u   u
u   u   u   u   u   u   u   u   u   u
u   u   u   u   u   u   u   u   u   u
u   u   u   u   u   u   u   u   u   u
˘   ˘   ˘   ˘   ˘   ˘   ˘   ˘   ˘   ˘
˘   ˘   ˘   ˘   ˘   ˘   ˘   ˘   ˘   ˘
˘   ˘   ˘   ˘   ˘   ˘   ˘   ˘   ˘   ˘
˘   ˘   ˘   ˘   ˘   ˘   ˘   ˘   ˘   ˘
...   .
...   .
...   .
...   .
...   .
.   .   .   .

Figure 4b 'Aurora'

have full regard for the role of chance and arbitrariness, which means thinking from the outside in at the same time as from the inside out.

Since ludic translation is by definition ergodic, the textual problem presented by a concrete poem can yield more than one solution. On this understanding, my

Solar

solar solar solar solar solar solar solar solar solar solar solar solar
solar solar solar solar solar solar solar solar solar solar solar solar
solar solar solar solar solar solar solar solar solar solar solar solar
solar solar solar solar solar solar solar solar solar solar solar solar
solar solar solar solar solar solar solar solar solar solar solar solar
solar solar solar solar solar solar solar solar solar solar solar solar
s o l s o l s o l s o l s o l s o l s o l s o l s o l s o l s o l s o l
s o l s o l s o l s o l s o l s o l s o l s o l s o l s o l s o l s o l
s o l s o l s o l s o l s o l s o l s o l s o l s o l s o l s o l s o l
s o l s o l s o l s o l s o l s o l s o l s o l s o l s o l s o l s o l
s o l s o l s o l s o l s o l s o l s o l s o l s o l s o l s o l s o l
s o l s o l s o l s o l s o l s o l s o l s o l s o l s o l s o l s o l
0   0   0   0   0   0   0   0   0   0   0   0
0   0   0   0   0   0   0   0   0   0   0   0
0   0   0   0   0   0   0   0   0   0   0   0
0   0   0   0   0   0   0   0   0   0   0   0
0   0   0   0   0   0   0   0   0   0   0   0
ᵕ   ᵕ   ᵕ   ᵕ   ᵕ   ᵕ   ᵕ   ᵕ   ᵕ   ᵕ   ᵕ   ᵕ
ᵕ   ᵕ   ᵕ   ᵕ   ᵕ   ᵕ   ᵕ   ᵕ   ᵕ   ᵕ   ᵕ   ᵕ
ᵕ   ᵕ   ᵕ   ᵕ   ᵕ   ᵕ   ᵕ   ᵕ   ᵕ   ᵕ   ᵕ   ᵕ
ᵕ   ᵕ   ᵕ   ᵕ   ᵕ   ᵕ   ᵕ   ᵕ   ᵕ   ᵕ   ᵕ   ᵕ
... .
... .
... .
... .
... .
.   .   .   .

Figure 4c 'Solar'

assistant and I attempted two further variations for 'White', each of which stages the 'moving light' meme using the same methodology but on the basis of a different set of resources. One variation, shown in Figure 4c, starts with 'solar', which links directly into the 'sun' theme in the Chinese original. 'Solar' then shrinks into 'sol', which is 'sun' in Latin and the name of the Roman sun god – this connection with ancient mythology also recalls the classical etymology underlying 'Aurora', providing a substrate recognizability between the two translations. And because of how 'sol' is spelt, it devolves into a vertical line of 'o' instead of 'u', as in the 'Aurora' translation. The rest of this variation follows 'Aurora' and the piece is retitled 'Solar' following its leading keyword.

The next variation, shown in Figure 4d, begins with a surprising choice of word: 'sunyata', which in Sanskrit means 'emptiness', thereby taking us on a completely different track than 'aurora' and 'solar'. The term 'sunyata' alludes to an instruction on meditation from the Buddhist text 'Explication on the sixteen visualizations', roughly translating as: 'How does one visualize? All sentient beings with eyes that are not born blind have seen the setting sun. One should sit properly, facing the west, and visualize that the sun is setting'.[19] On the level of form, 'sunyata' is felicitous because it boils down easily to 'sun' in line with the original theme, although the 'sun' in 'sunyata' is etymologically unrelated to the English word 'sun', and because 'sun' contains a 'u' we could further develop the rest of the poem the way we did with 'Aurora'.

For our purpose, the important point about this last variation is that it was the brainchild of my assistant, who happened to be a Buddhist. As we were working in ludic mode, my assistant took his religious sensibilities into our reimagining of the Chinese poem. More specifically, in recalling a Buddhist text on medita-tion while translating Chen Li's poem, he was effectively performing a radial reading – even though we did not have this technical term at that point – where the theme of visualizing the setting sun as captured in the Buddhist text is brought to bear on the meme of moving light in 'White'.

Together the three translations above demonstrate how a meme from Chen Li's poem is ludically translated by way of being re-entextualized in multiple manifestations. The original meme constitutes a nexus through which the three variations share an intertextual, substrate recognizability on the level of the gestalt, even if the discrete signs in the source text ('white', 'day', and so forth) are not directly traceable in the translations. Such memicity (*not* mimicry) is the basis of ludic translation, whereby the concept of a poem, not its lexico-grammatical signs, constitutes a mobile element that disseminates across and holds together different articulations of a text. Each of these articulations plays out 'textual adjustments' that reset the meme 'in different frames of meaning and use' (Varis & Blommaert 2015: 37), such that the relation between a translation and its original can be said to be *uncanny* – formally different yet still familiar at some level. Together, the three variations

---

[19] This line is translated by Steven W. K. Chan from a Chinese version of the Buddhist text.

Sunyata

sunyata sunyata sunyata sunyata sunyata sunyata sunyata sunyata sunyata sunyata
sunyata sunyata sunyata sunyata sunyata sunyata sunyata sunyata sunyata sunyata
sunyata sunyata sunyata sunyata sunyata sunyata sunyata sunyata sunyata sunyata
sunyata sunyata sunyata sunyata sunyata sunyata sunyata sunyata sunyata sunyata
sunyata sunyata sunyata sunyata sunyata sunyata sunyata sunyata sunyata sunyata
sunyata sunyata sunyata sunyata sunyata sunyata sunyata sunyata sunyata sunyata

sun	sun	sun	sun	sun	sun	sun	sun	sun	sun
sun	sun	sun	sun	sun	sun	sun	sun	sun	sun
sun	sun	sun	sun	sun	sun	sun	sun	sun	sun
sun	sun	sun	sun	sun	sun	sun	sun	sun	sun
sun	sun	sun	sun	sun	sun	sun	sun	sun	sun
sun	sun	sun	sun	sun	sun	sun	sun	sun	sun
u	u	u	u	u	u	u	u	u	u
u	u	u	u	u	u	u	u	u	u
u	u	u	u	u	u	u	u	u	u
u	u	u	u	u	u	u	u	u	u
u	u	u	u	u	u	u	u	u	u
‿	‿	‿	‿	‿	‿	‿	‿	‿	‿
‿	‿	‿	‿	‿	‿	‿	‿	‿	‿
‿	‿	‿	‿	‿	‿	‿	‿	‿	‿
‿	‿	‿	‿	‿	‿	‿	‿	‿	‿
...	...	...	...	...	...	...	...	...	...
...	...	...	...	...	...	...	...	...	...
...	...	...	...	...	...	...	...	...	...
...	...	...	...	...	...	...	...	...	...
...	...	...	...	...	...	...	...	...	...
.	.	.	.	.	.	.	.	.	.

Figure 4d 'Sunyata'

coalesce into a text-complex that prosthetically extends the original poem into something larger than itself.

Although the three variations above are presented as English translations, they are in fact heteroglossic in their constitution, featuring Latin ('Aurora' and

'Solar') and Sanskrit ('Sunyata'). Insofar as Chen Li's original work does not contain languages other than Chinese (although it does contain non-verbal shapes, as do the translations), such heteroglossia can be seen as a surplus produced in translation, a value-adding feature that does not originate in the source text. This suggests that from a ludic perspective, translation does more than substitute one language code with another; it mobilizes resources in relation to different frames of meaning and use, exceeding the boundaries of named languages (English, Chinese, Latin) and, as we shall see below, of language as such.

Perhaps the most important quality of ludic translation highlighted by these three variations is the indeterminacy of the process. In conceiving these translations I catered for a degree of randomness, allowing for radial strands of thinking and reading from outside the poem to interact with its meme. Hence, the three translations can be seen as the tentative result of my (and my assistant's) repeated engagement with the poem's meme using, among other things, our own experience with and knowledge of light-related discourses (aura photos, polar lights) that lie outside the text.

The ensuing experience stands in contrast with that of straight translation, characterized by the ordered and rational transference of meaning, perhaps clause by clause or line by line, from one language into another. Experimental translation is much more chaotic, idiosyncratic, and unpredictable, continually inflected by epiphanic images and texts conjured up in the here-and-now of translating. Instead of discarding these idiosyncrasies and epiphanies as irrelevant to the work of translation, a ludic perspective embraces them and actively considers how they can be co-opted to add value to the original work in unexpected ways.

What this means is that each time a work is translated, even by the same translator, the outcome will inevitably be different because the extraneous circumstances impinging on each instance of translation can never be exactly the same. My translations therefore do not represent a final resolution of Chen's poem. Potentially any number of variations in any number of languages can be churned out of the same meme, depending on a host of contingent factors, such as the resources available in a particular target repertoire as well as the translator's capacity in accessing those resources. The gamic character of the translating process lies precisely in an experimental search for a feasible, though necessarily partial, solution using the resources at one's disposal.

The resources available for use in translation are not necessarily linguistic. We have seen that the three translations in Figures 4b–d perform an attrition in alphabetic strings to translate the aggregated patterning in the original poem based on the successive decomposition of the Chinese character for 'white'. One consequence of this approach, as noted above, is that the angular shape of the original poem is compromised mid-way. This is not necessarily a drawback as such, because every performative translation foregrounds certain aspects of a text while backgrounding other aspects depending on the available semiotic resources. The formal shift is part of the performance. The question then arises as to how we can transcreate the poem's meme using alternative resources so that the integrity of its original shape is maintained.

On this note, I present one last variation on 'White', which pivots toward the paralinguistic device of colour (Figure 4e). Since it is determined that the meme of the original poem is about changing intensities of illumination, I chose 'light' as the keyword for the translation, which also makes it the title of the translated poem. The word is replicated many times over to form a rectangular shape and then divided into different segments according to the vertical development pattern in the original (six rows – six rows – five rows – four rows – three rows – two rows – one row). Using the gradient function (adjusting for 'attribute', 'angle', 'stop') within the Adobe application InDesign, I applied to each segment a black colouring at a different point on the saturation scale, defined as 'the scale from the most intense, pure manifestation of a colour to "chromatic grey," a grey with just a tinge of that colour, and ultimately to complete desaturation, achromatic grey' (van Leeuwen 2022: 84).

In multimodal semiotics, saturation scales represent the continuum from 'maximum emotive intensity to maximally restrained, maximally toned-down emotion', which can attract 'more precise meanings and values' in context (van Leeuwen 2022: 84). In the context of 'White', this saturation scale can be used to signify different intensities of brightness, from maximally intensive to maximally toned-down. In applying different saturation scales across layered tiers of the word 'light', my translation creates a gradual transformation on the reading interface from intense black (strong light) through chromatic grey (waning light) to achromatic grey (faint light), hence replaying the original poem's meme using visual rather than verbal resources.

The Paralinguistics of Translation: 'Pyramid in Flames'

My next example further illustrates how ludic translation can draw on paralinguistic resources to offer a multimodal interpretation of the source text. The poem in question is Chen Li's 'Photo of Egyptian Scenery in the Dream of a Fire Department Captain', shown in Figure 5a. The text is in the shape of a pyramid, which comprises repetitions of the character 火 (*huo*, 'fire'). The title gives us

Light

light light light light light light light light light light light light light light light light light
light light light light light light light light light light light light light light light light light
light light light light light light light light light light light light light light light light light
light light light light light light light light light light light light light light light light light
light light light light light light light light light light light light light light light light light
light light light light light light light light light light light light light light light light light
light light light light light light light light light light light light light light light light light
light light light light light light light light light light light light light light light light light
light light light light light light light light light light light light light light light light light
light light light light light light light light light light light light light light light light light
light light light light light light light light light light light light light light light light light
light light light light light light light light light light light light light light light light light
light light light light light light light light light light light light light light light light light
light light light light light light light light light light light light light light light light light
light light light light light light light light light light light light light light light light light
light light light light light light light light light light light light light light light light light
light light light light light light light light light light light light light light light light light
light light light light light light light light light light light light light light light light light
light light light light light light light light light light light light light light light light light
light light light light light light light light light light light light light light light light light
light light light light light light light light light light light light light light light light light

Figure 4e 'Light'

the interpretive key: we are in a fire captain's dreamscape in which an Egyptian pyramid is in flames. The 'fire' character seems to lend itself easily to straight translation. Such a translation, in which each occurrence of 火 is substituted by its literal translation, was attempted by Chang Fen-ling and appears on Chen

消防隊長夢中的埃及風景照

火
火火火
火火火火火
火火火火火火火
火火火火火火火火火
火火火火火火火火火火火
火火火火火火火火火火火火火
火火火火火火火火火火火火火火火
火火火火火火火火火火火火火火火火火
火火火火火火火火火火火火火火火火火火火
火火火火火火火火火火火火火火火火火火火火火
火火火火火火火火火火火火火火火火火火火火火火火
火火火火火火火火火火火火火火火火火火火火火火火火火
火火火火火火火火火火火火火火火火火火火火火火火火火火火
火火火火火火火火火火火火火火火火火火火火火火火火火火火火火
火火火火火火火火火火火火火火火火火火火火火火火火火火火火火火火
火火火火火火火火火火火火火火火火火火火火火火火火火火火火火火火火火
火火火火火火火火火火火火火火火火火火火火火火火火火火火火火火火火火火火
火火火火火火火火火火火火火火火火火火火火火火火火火火火火火火火火火火火火火

Figure 5a Original text of ‘Photo of Egyptian Scenery in the Dream of a Fire Department Captain’

Photo of Egyptian Scenery in the Dream of a Fire Department Captain

fire
firefirefire
firefirefirefirefire
firefirefirefirefirefirefire
firefirefirefirefirefirefirefirefire
firefirefirefirefirefirefirefirefirefirefire
firefirefirefirefirefirefirefirefirefirefirefirefire
firefirefirefirefirefirefirefirefirefirefirefirefirefirefire
firefirefirefirefirefirefirefirefirefirefirefirefirefirefirefirefire
firefirefirefirefirefirefirefirefirefirefirefirefirefirefirefirefirefirefire
firefirefirefirefirefirefirefirefirefirefirefirefirefirefirefirefirefirefirefirefire
firefirefirefirefirefirefirefirefirefirefirefirefirefirefirefirefirefirefirefirefirefirefire
firefirefirefirefirefirefirefirefirefirefirefirefirefirefirefirefirefirefirefirefirefirefirefirefire
firefirefirefirefirefirefirefirefirefirefirefirefirefirefirefirefirefirefirefirefirefirefirefirefirefirefire

Figure 5b English translation of 'Photo of Egyptian Scenery in the Dream of a Fire Department Captain' by Chang Fen-ling

Pyramid in Flames: A Fire Captain's Dream

fla
red*fla*red*fla*
red*fla*red*fla*red*fla*
red*fla*red*fla*red*fla*red*fla*
red*fla*red*fla*red*fla*red*fla*red*fla*
red*fla*red*fla*red*fla*red*fla*red*fla*red*fla*
red*fla*red*fla*red*fla*red*fla*red*fla*red*fla*red*fla*
red*fla*red*fla*red*fla*red*fla*red*fla*red*fla*red*fla*red*fla*
red*fla*red*fla*red*fla*red*fla*red*fla*red*fla*red*fla*red*fla*red*fla*
red*fla*red*fla*red*fla*red*fla*red*fla*red*fla*red*fla*red*fla*red*fla*red*fla*
red*fla*red*fla*red*fla*red*fla*red*fla*red*fla*red*fla*red*fla*red*fla*red*fla*red*fla*
red*fla*red*fla*red*fla*red*fla*red*fla*red*fla*red*fla*red*fla*red*fla*red*fla*red*fla*red*fla*
red*fla*red*fla*red*fla*red*fla*red*fla*red*fla*red*fla*red*fla*red*fla*red*fla*red*fla*red*fla*red*fla*
red*fla*red*fla*red*fla*red*fla*red*fla*red*fla*red*fla*red*fla*red*fla*red*fla*red*fla*red*fla*red*fla*red*fla*
red*fla*red*fla*red*fla*red*fla*red*fla*red*fla*red*fla*red*fla*red*fla*red*fla*red*fla*red*fla*red*fla*red*fla*red*fla*
red*fla*red*fla*red*fla*red*fla*red*fla*red*fla*red*fla*red*fla*red*fla*red*fla*red*fla*red*fla*red*fla*red*fla*red*fla*red*fla*

Figure 5c 'Pyramid in Flames: A Fire Captain's Dream'

Li's official website (see Figure 5b). In *The Edge of the Island*, however, Chang adopted her usual strategy of non-translation (Chen 2014: 170), leaving the Chinese characters as they are while closely translating the title. A footnote, which reads 'The Chinese character 火=fire; 焱=flames' is added to the base of the translation.

This explanatory footnote, which does not appear in the Chinese original, not only points to the source of the poem's perceived untranslatability; it effectively cancels the validity of the straight translation in Figure 5b.[20] As it turns out, the constitution of Chen Li's original pyramid of 'fire' characters is more sophisticated than it appears. It does not simply juxtapose repetitions of the same character but plays with extendable reading frames generated by the architectonics of the Chinese ideograph. More precisely: if we zoom into a discrete occurrence of 火 in the pyramid, we get the character for 'fire'; if we broaden our lens slightly and observe two of the same character stacked one on top of the other, we get 炎 (*yan*), which means 'inflammation' or 'burning hot'. Triangulating three 'fire' characters gives us 焱 (*yan*), or 'bright flame', while squaring four of these characters produces 燚 (*yi*), meaning 'enormous flames'.

Taken together, the four etymologically-related ideographs fan out a range of intensities around the 'fire' motif, signifying the modulation of heat during a conflagration. Yet when meshed into the space of the pyramid, their boundaries become indistinct. The aesthetic point of the poem – its meme – is precisely for us to visualize the four characters into being and appreciate how the invisible frames of these characters recursively embed one another. In other words, readers in the know, that is, readers with some knowledge of Chinese writing, are invited to identify the overlapping aggregated patternings beneath the surface manifestation of the word-pyramid.

The prospective English readers of my translation are, of course, not in the know; and they are not serviced by the straight translation in Figure 5b, in which the word ('fire') is duly translated but the meme of recursive reading frames is lost. Losing the meme of a concrete poem is as good as not translating at all, and that justifies a retranslation. To recuperate the meme in my retranslation, I (together with my research assistant again) started thinking obliquely, with a view to finding two or more English keywords that fulfil two criteria: first, in keeping with the overall theme of the source text, they should be within the semantic field of 'fire', though they need not literally mean 'fire'; second, they can recursively embed each other into overlapping reading frames. The first of

---

[20] My hypothesis is that Chang Fen-ling attempted the straight translation for Chen Li's website first, failing which she decided to go with non-translation and paratextual treatment for the print collection *The Edge of the Island*.

these criteria is linguistic; the second is paralinguistic as it takes the visual patterning of verbal strings into consideration.

First, we churned out four candidate keywords that fulfil the first criterion, namely 'flame', 'torch', 'blaze', and 'flare'. Then, we looked closely at these words and considered whether adding one or more words could turn them into a recursive string. In retrospect, this process was affectively akin to playing Scrambles. We brainstormed many possibilities, most of which proved futile until we angled on the dimension of colour. Chen Li's poem is black and white but we asked how his pyramid might have looked in the imaginary dreamscape of the fire captain. Assuming that its colour would have been between dark orange and red, we experimented with the X+flame, X+torch, X+blaze, X+flare collocations, substituting 'orange' and 'red' for X in each case.

It was when we arrived at the collocation 'red flare' that we knew we had hit on a potential keyword. As a noun phrase, 'red flare' refers to a handheld device giving off distress signals, which ties in with the fire theme of the poem. The *re-* in 'red' and the *-re* in 'flare' could be capitalized upon to create a recursive string to fulfil the second criterion. We immediately put pen to paper, stringing together several occurrences of 'red flare', closing the gap between the two words, hence: 'redflare redflare redflare redflare'. We then conflated the overlapping *-re-* between the successive strings to create a continuous reading. The word 'flare' now meshes into 'red', unexpectedly producing the intermediary word 'flared', which is the past participle of the verb 'flare' (as in 'flared up') and thus also relates to the conflagration theme at hand. The resulting string becomes 'redflaredflaredflaredflared', recursively embedding 'red', 'flare', and 'flared'.

Figure 5c shows my translation, retitled 'Pyramid in Flames: A Fire Captain's Dream', a tad less of a mouthful and a more idiomatic version of Chang's English title. The translation re-entextualizes the meme of the Chinese original using a new constellation of signs, playing with the same visual idea of embedding character frames but with recourse to alphabetic strings. In this process, the translation refurnishes the Chinese poem. For example, the materiality of colour is central to my translation but does not figure in the Chinese original. The possibility of jamming 'red' with 'flare' together into a recursive string is also incidental to the orthographic and grammatical affordances of English. Because of its ludic nature, my translation does not, and cannot, represent a definitive version of Chen Li's poem, even in English. A different target language may (or may not) offer yet another set of affordances, which would facilitate (or impede) an articulation of the meme along a different trajectory, with its own value-adding features.

To foreground the concept of colour, which represents the semiotic excess brought forth by the translation, I decided to colour the embedded word 'red' in red in all its occurrences. This dramatizes the fire captain's dreamscape as enacted in the translation, bringing the image of conflagration more vividly into readers' sight. It also serves to segment the string and highlight the meme of overlapping and recursive reading. This latter effect is further accentuated with my italicization of the *fla* in 'flared' to mimic the dynamic movement of flames. Together, these two paralinguistic interventions generate visual modulation, adding theatrical value to an otherwise static, black and white poem. It is granted that these visual embellishments are much less florid and random than those featured in the transcreative work of Clive Scott (see Figure 1). Nevertheless, in heightening the target text's sensory interface, my translation seeks to improvise on Chen Li's poem in a way that takes it beyond its verbal signs toward a performative, multimodal trajectory. As such, my translation can be seen as a more subdued version of Scott's synaesthetic translation, which resists the 'disembodiment of text' and returns the latter instead 'to a full, proliferating materiality' (Scott 2019: 98).

Memesis across Media: 'Insects for Breakfast'

The preceding example demonstrates a key difference between ludic and straight translation: rather than *words* and *languages*, ludic translation is based around *resources* and *repertoires*. Whereas straight translation aims at transiting a work from one language code into another, ludic translation goes beyond language as such to orchestrate the full extent of available and accessible resources, including non-verbal ones like colour and typography, in meaning-making. A ludic perspective on translation foregrounds multimodal performativity over and above the discursive signification of an original work.

Pushing further beyond multimodality, the next set of examples illustrates memesis across media, in which a written poem is translated in ludic style and resemiotized beyond print. Figure 6a shows Chen Li's 'Breakfast Tablecloth of a Solitary Entomologist'. The poem comprises a rectangular block of characters that share a common radical, the pictograph 虫 (*chong*, 'insect'). What may be slightly surprising is that the poem cannot be, or at any rate is not meant to be, read. Each of the 'insect' characters can be found in a Chinese dictionary and are therefore technically pronounceable. Yet many of them, particularly the orthographically complex ones toward the bottom of the rectangular block, are highly obscure such as to be hardly recognizable or readable to the Chinese native speaker. These characters are visually familiar in their material constitution yet

孤獨昆蟲學家的早餐桌巾

虰虮虬虰虱豹虴虷虹虳虵虼蚅蚆蚇蚊
蚋蚌蚍蚎蚐蚑蚓蚔蚕蚖蚗蚘蚙蚚蚜蚝
蚞蚡蚢蚣蚤蚊蚧蚨蚩蚪蚳蚰蚱蚲蚴蚵
蚶蚷蚸蚹蚺蚻蚼蚾蚿蛀蛁蛂蛃蛄蛅蛆
蛈蛇蛉蛋蛌蛍蛑蛓蛔蛕蛗蛘蛙蛚蛛
蛜蛝蛞蛟蛜蛣蛤蛦蛨蛩蛪蛬蛭蛯蛵
蛷蛸蛹蛺蛻蛾蜀蜁蜂蜃蜄蜅蜆蜇蜋蜍
蜊蜋蜌蜎蜐蜑蜓蜒蜘蜙蜚蜛蜜蜞蜠蜡
蜢蜣蜤蜥蜦蜨蜩蜪蜫蜬蜮蜯蜰蜱蜲蜳
蜴蜵蜷蜸蜺蜻蜼蜾蜿蝀蝁蝂蝃蝄蝅蝆
蝎蝏蝐蝑蝒蝓蝔蝕蝖蝗蝘蝙蝚蝛蝜蝝
蝞蝟蝠蝡蝢蝣蝤蝥蝦蝧蝨蝩蝪蝫蝬蝭
蝮蝯蝰蝱蝲蝴蝵蝶蝷蝸蝹蝺蝻蝼蝽蝾
蝿螀螁螂螃螄 螇螉螊螌融螎螏螐螑螒
螓螔螕螖螗螘螙螚螛螜螝螞螟螠螡螢
螣螤螥螦螧螨螩螪螫螬螭螮 螯
螰螱螲螳螴螵螶螷螸螹螺螻螼螽螾螿
蟀蟁蟂蟃蟄蟅蟆蟇蟈蟉蟊蟋蟌蟍蟎
蟏蟐蟑蟒蟓蟔蟕蟖蟗蟘蟙蟚蟛蟜蟝蟞
蟟蟠蟡蟢蟣蟤蟥蟦 蟧蟨蟩蟪蟫蟬蟭
蟮蟯蟰蟱蟲蟳蟴蟵蟶蟷蟸蟹蟺蟻蟼蟽
蟾蟿蠀蠁 蠂蠃蠄蠅蠆蠇 蠈蠉蠊蠋
蠌蠍蠎蠏蠐蠑蠒蠓蠔蠕蠖蠗蠘蠙蠚蠛

Figure 6a Original text of 'Breakfast Tablecloth of a Solitary Entomologist'

elusive in meaning, belonging as they do to the technical-scientific register of entomology.

As with much of Chen Li's concrete poetry, we are faced with a text in which there is more to be seen than to be read. The title suggests we are looking at a piece of tablecloth whose owner is an insect expert. In this visual context, the characters, each of which has a different verbal meaning of its own, signify as individual icons accruing into a larger grotesque image: a tablecloth crawled over by insects. A few interesting observations can be made of the Chinese text. First, the constellation is punctuated by a number of blank spaces; if we are looking at a tablecloth, then these signify holes bitten through by the insect-characters. Second, the Chinese characters appear to be vertically arranged in increasing order of complexity; those at the bottom tiers are much more sophisticated in structure and contain more strokes than those in the upper tiers.

Lastly, a number of the characters denote creatures other than insects, for instance 蛇 (*she*, 'snake') and 蟹 (*xie*, 'crab'), or even non-living things, such as 蠢 (*chun*, 'foolish'). Because they too carry the 'insect' component, they are camouflaged among the other characters even though they do not denote insects. Their inclusion in the visual matrix points to the non-verbality of the text as a whole, in which the characters signify through their form rather than meaning. And the fact that many of the characters, especially those appearing in the bottom tiers, can barely be understood – without recourse to a dictionary, that is – further amplifies their corporeality. Their unutterability partakes of the work's signification.

Once again, the poem is implicitly pronounced untranslatable in *The Edge of the Island*, appearing in its original form except for its title, which is closely translated into English (Chen 2014: 171). If the individual signs in the original Chinese text are intended to both entice readers (in terms of a familiar orthography) and elude them (in terms of their undecipherability), then a straight translation would surely be counterproductive. Enter ludic translation with its focus on the meme, which I would formulate as 'a visual monstrosity created through the alienation of language'. The original text, as we have seen, defamiliarizes the Chinese script by putting together obscure characters sharing a common 'insect' radical. Thinking obliquely, the ludic translator would ask: what kind of script would have a similar alienating effect for English readers?

Considering we are dealing with an entomological theme, Latin quickly comes to mind. As is well known, insects have scientific appellations in Latin in addition to their common names. And because Latin uses the alphabetic script, it is orthographically consonant with English, many of whose words can be traced to Latin roots. Yet as a language, Latin is unfamiliar to most contemporary users of English, its usage restricted to more specialized domains in academia. More specifically, scientific appellations in Latin are generally long and complicated in spelling as compared with modern English. Prima facie, they offer the visual affordances to develop into monstrous and alienating linguistic formations for English-language readers and are a felicitous resource for our purpose.

With this in mind, my assistant and I set out to translate the 'insect' characters in Chen Li's poem into Latin, by which I do not mean finding the Latin equivalent for each character – that would derive a straight translation that is ultimately meaningless precisely because of its interest in meaning. Rather, we wanted to create the work anew, keeping its meme of monstrosity and alienation while altogether side-tracking its signs. From the word 'ento-mologist', based on Chang's translation of the original Chinese title, we googled and found the official website of the Entomological Society of America,[21] which hosts a large online database of insect names. We elicited from the database a corpus of scientific names of insects, from which we selected a smaller number to be arranged into the shape of a rectangle tablecloth.

We laid out the Latin words in alphabetical order of their first letter, starting with *archatina* on the top left to *yumensis* on the bottom right. This was meant as a response to the original arrangement of Chinese characters, which became increasingly complicated in terms of their number of strokes as one moves from the top to the bottom of the 'tablecloth'. Following the Chinese original, we also randomly deleted some words to create insect-bitten 'holes' in the text; the exact placement of those holes is immaterial in the context of the poem. Finally, I tried out a few font types for the lettering and decided on `Consolas`, whose slightly archaic, typewriter-style contour evokes – for me, that is – the 'feel' of insect tentacles as compared with other sans serif fonts. In ludic translation, font type is a parameter that can be tweaked for desired effects – recall Clive Scott's translation in Figure 1 with its juxtaposition of several fonts.

Figure 6b shows my transcreation of Chen Li's poem, which is mostly Latin save for the English title. I find the original title translated by Chang Fen-ling unwieldy. We came up with a couple of candidates like 'Breakfast with the Insects', suggesting that the entomologist is eating breakfast while his insects are on the table. This option would have omitted the tablecloth and entomologist themes, which are essential for interpreting the text's contour as a tablecloth festering with insects. Even the word 'solitary' is key in indicating the dispos-ition of the scientist who, in my readerly imagination, might have neglected to do housekeeping (hence insects crawling over the tablecloth) and, more gorily, might even have developed the macabre habit of eating insects for breakfast in his solitary moments. This would give rise to a different interpretation for the holes in the tablecloth.

---

[21] www.entsoc.org

Insects for Breakfast:
A Lonely Entomologist's Tablecloth

achatina amygdali asahinai atriceps bambusae
biformis boninsis brevipes   bullatus
buoliana calabaza carinata catalpae chalybea
citrulli claviger clavipes comptana confusus
cornutus crataegi cribrata declivis demoleus
dominica   elliotti elotella eriosoma
exitiosa fagisuga femorata figurans flavipes
funebris fuscella gallinae geminata gibbosus
gloverii gossypii graminis graminum hammondi
hebesana hesperus   illucens inodorus
inornata irritans jeffreyi juniperi lantanae
laticeps lecontei legitima limitata lineatum
longulus maculata maricopa melanura modestus
morrilli   nyctalis oblinita obovatus
obscurus occiduus oleivora packardi palmarum
paludosa persicae phaseoli pictipes princeps
purchasi pyricola radiatae raphanus ribearia
rigidana robiniae rugglesi   salticus
scalaris scandens schwarzi seriatus sericeus
          sinuatus stevensi suspensa tenellus
tokionis topiaria trigonum ulmicola vaccinii
vandykei vicarius viticida websteri yumensis

Figure 6b 'Insects for Breakfast'

I decided to retitle my English version 'Insects for Breakfast: A Lonely
Entomologist's Tablecloth'. I changed 'solitary' to 'lonely' to foreground an

emotional dimension in the entomologist's life that better conveys the affect of the Chinese adjective 孤獨 (*gudu*) in the original title. The preposition 'for' is meant as a placeholder. I initially used 'at', suggesting co-location: we might, for instance, imagine the entomologist breakfasting in front of his table covered with a cloth strewn with crawling insects. But this scenario is too 'mild' for my taste, and this is where my personality and disposition as a risk-taking translator enter the picture. So I experimented with other prepositions ('for', 'with', 'among'), each of which would give rise to a slightly different story. I finally decided on 'for' because there is something grotesque in the implication that the obsessed entomologist, being cooped up in his home or laboratory alone all the time, has started developing a habit of breakfasting on his research objects. This reading is of course not attested in Chen Li's original title; it is purely a translational intervention based on my extrapolative thinking.

But is it not a misnomer to call this an *English* translation when in fact the body text comprises entirely of Latin terms? Perhaps this is a wrong question to ask in the first place, for it is not the identity of the target language that matters here. We are not so much translating into Latin per se as using Latin as a resource repertoire to develop the meme of the Chinese poem. Instead of restricting our imaginary of translation to a point-to-point correspondence between two closed language systems, ludic translation opens up the discursive space to the full gamut of linguistic and semiotic resources available to the translator. These resources can be orchestrated across their perceived boundaries, for instance, Latin versus English or text versus colour/typography, so as to enrich the heteroglossic and multimodal texture of translation.

My experiment with Chen Li's Chinese insects could very well have ended here but that would mean discarding a large number of Latin names harvested from the entomological database. With the notion of resemiotization in mind, we further experimented with the idea of transposing our version into an electronic platform in a way that might enable us to recycle those remaining terms in our corpus, perhaps in a random, ergodic manner. At this juncture, the tabular design of Chen Li's poem, within which characters are lined up in neat files, calls to our minds the celled interface of Microsoft Excel. Thus, we tried transferring our corpus of names collected from the database into an Excel spreadsheet. Using the functions INDEX and RANDBETWEEN, we created a dynamic interface out of the corpus, as shown in Figure 6c. This interface can be intervened in by the reader, who can generate random constellations of words on the screen by placing a cursor on any empty cell in the spreadsheet and clicking the Delete key.

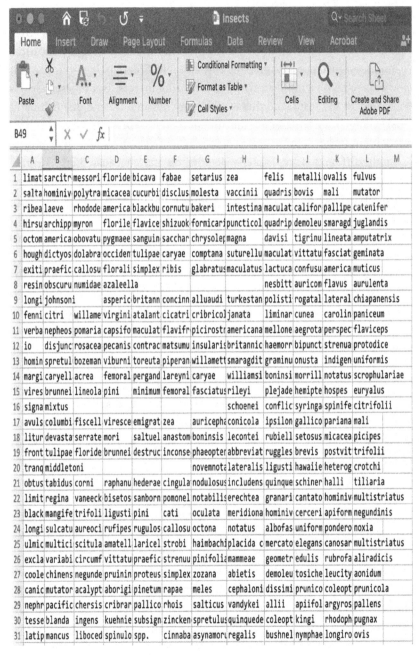

Figure 6c Excel-mediated version of 'Insects for Breakfast'

In resemiotizing Chen Li's poem into an electronic interface, we have essentially turned the original work into a *cybertext*, both in the ordinary sense of a digitally-mediated text and in Aarseth's (1997) sense of a manoeuvrable, co-constructive text.[22] Whereas in their print format, both Chen Li's original poem and my translation consist of a given, unchangeable set of characters that is primarily visual, our Excel version transforms the written text into a digital artefact whose outcome can be influenced by readerly interception (Aarseth 1997: 4). The resemiotized poem now invites the reader to engage with it visually but also kinetically, hence introducing an ergodic element and turning poetry reading into an embodied, gamic event. As a result, an almost unlimited number of permutations of insect names can be generated to create a virtual, dynamic 'tablecloth'. The Excel translation generates flux and randomness to the poem's reading interface, producing a text-machine that can churn out multiple variations on Chen's poem at the click of a mouse button.

In this set of examples, I have developed the meme in Chen Li's poem across languages and extended it into a different medial dimension via two operations of translation. The first transits Chinese characters into the Latin alphabet; the second re-mediates a text in print into a spreadsheet in Microsoft Excel. The former is interlingual, the latter, transmedial, where an already translated text transcends media platforms, taking on 'an entirely new set of contextualization conditions' (Varis & Blommaert 2015: 36) provided by Microsoft Excel. As we have seen, Excel offers the affordances, realized through formulaic commands, to unsettle a static configuration of signs in flux. In other words, as the translated poem moves through Microsoft Excel, it undergoes an 'entirely "new" semiotic process, allowing new semiotic modes and resources to be involved in the repetition process' (Varis & Blommaert 2015: 36).

Such resemiotization changes the way in which the text is navigated, with the reader having more embodied and ergodic agency in the Excel-mediated version than in the print version. Navigational functionalities, as Hayles (2005: 90–1) reminds us, 'are not merely ways to access the work but part of a work's signifying structure'. To change the navigational potentialities of Chen Li's poem through Excel's resemiotization is, therefore, to change the work materially. This change in materiality is what Hayles (2005: 116) calls media translation, one performing 'conjunctions' between 'print and electronic textualities'. In this last

---

[22] In Aarseth's (1997) terms, a cybertext, be it digital or non-digital, is 'a work of physical construction', in which readers participate by 'effectua[ting] a semiotic sequence' by means of 'a selective movement' (1). This takes us back to the notion of ergodicity which, as defined earlier, means 'non-trivial' work is required on the reader's part in engaging the text, meaning reading efforts that go beyond 'eye movement and the periodic or arbitrary turning of pages' (2). For example, readers can intervene in the surface-level manifestation of a poem, such as setting it in a sequence of morphing transformations, through text input or mouse-over (Montfort 2001). The digital art of John Cayley (see discussion earlier) exemplifies the cybertext in both its conventional and theoretical senses, often with a translational twist.

usage, translation is appropriated as a metaphor to highlight the material constitution of a work, which must transform as the work moves from one medium to another.

My transposition of 'Insects for Breakfast' in Excel, conservative as it may be in technical sophistication, aligns with transmedial developments in Chen Li's oeuvre. The poet has a YouTube channel[23] that houses varied performances based around his work, including recitals, musical renditions, and ambient videos. A symbiotic relationship obtains between a poem as it appears in print and as it is performed in other modes and media; each complements the other by capturing an experiential aspect of the work. For example, 'A War Symphony' (see Figure 2) has at least two media spin-offs, an animated version and a recital version.[24] The animated version by Wu Hsiu-ching dramatizes the poem into a virtual battle, splitting the textual configuration of the original into two mobile masses of 兵 characters, whose two 'limbs' at the bottom are made to move left and right in emulation of marching soldiers. The two armies are coded blue and red, and as they collide on screen, we see 兵 characters from both sides striking out the 'limbs' of their opponents into 乒 and 乓. And when these characters lose their only remaining limb, they turn into a 丘 in black. The animation concludes with a black and white display of 乒, 乓, and 丘 sprawled out and overlapping one another like a pile of debris. Hence, this animated version adds value to the poem by way of the kinetic and colour-coding of the Chinese characters, which are made possible by virtue of the affordances of its medium.

The recital version by Chen Li himself is value-adding in a different way. The oral-aural nuances afforded by Chen's reading give his poem a semiotic dimension that is at most latent in the printed text. In reading the poem himself, Chen Li imagines the elongated coda in *qiu* ('mound') as onomatopoeic of the 'eerie autumn winds': *zhenzhen guimei de qiufeng*, where *qiu* ('autumn') bears an ambivalent sound-meaning value (Chen Li, personal communication). Chen's rendition of *qiu* 丘 in an 'extended, lingering breath' can also be taken to suggest 'the last, languid breathing of dying soldiers' (Chiu 2018: 33). On this reading, the interaction between 'the spatiality of visual poetry and the temporality of sound poetry' (Chiu 2018: 33) extends 'A War Symphony' from a written text into a verbal-sonic assemblage.

The last two examples demonstrate how the discursive space of literary writing can be opened up to articulations across media platforms, creating semiotic outcomes that share a memic recognizability with the original text while affording it new expressive and affective capacities. They show that

---

[23] www.youtube.com/user/chenli103/videos

[24] Both versions can be viewed at www.youtube.com/watch?v=jZjj5y-7e9Q

translation can simultaneously be engaged in its substantive and tropic senses to explore the interlingual, multimodal, and transmedial dimensions of semiotic performance. Across all of these dimensions, translation stands in a ludic relation with the original not by directly treating its signs but instead by re-entextualizing and resemiotizing its memes.

3 Implications and Conclusions

This excursion in translating concrete poetry is meant as a provocation to think around the question of translatability and, ultimately, the ontology of literary expression. I recapitulate my main arguments as follows.

a. Ludic translation focuses on memes rather than signs. This releases the translator from the grip of discursive language, with the implication that a source text can potentially generate multiple transtextual solutions to an initial textual problem, including in the same target language. Each of these solutions can re-entextualize the meme of the source text in its own way by drawing on signifying resources available and accessible in the target repertoire. My four versions of the poem 'White' illustrate this point.

b. The resources drawn upon in ludic translation include linguistic and non-linguistic ones. The latter includes visual cues such as mannerisms of punctuation, colour, spacing, or typography, which serve to transform a verbal text into a multimodal artefact, as for instance 'Nation' and 'Pyramid in Flames'. Taking non-linearity to the extreme, a text's meme can also be resemiotized beyond the written page by tapping into the affordances of alternative platforms, thereby dovetailing translation with transmedial production. This is exemplified by the animated version of 'A War Symphony' and my Excel-mediated version of 'Insects for Breakfast'.

c. The object of ludic translation is to add performative value to a source text more than to transmit or communicate its instrumental meaning. It operates in ergodic mode, entailing non-trivial, and in my case also collaborative, translation effort beyond the linear transference of meaning from one language into another. In contrast to straight translation, which aims to ascertain the lexico-grammatical meaning of a source text and represent that meaning with precision and clarity, ludic translation opens up a text to playful experimentation. Such experimentation is moderated through the translator's knowledge, disposition, and subjectivity as well as their sensory and embodied experience of reading at a particular point in time and within a specific sociocultural milieu. It is translating by the seat of one's pants.

d. Ludic translation is contingent on all the material and non-material circumstances surrounding a translation event. It thrives on creative indeterminacy, taking us away from outcome-based thinking that focusses on a single, clear-cut, definitive solution to any given translation problem. Indeed, ludic translation embraces untranslatability itself as integral to the process of translating. Here translation failure is factored into a gamic vision of translation, which involves risks – as when translation is frustrated mid-way or when its outcome turns out to be unsatisfactory – as well as rewards – as, for instance, when a sudden epiphany leads to a viable solution and personal satisfaction. Ludic translators perform their practice as a wager and in gambit mode.

Revaluating Untranslatability

Ludic translation has implications for how we think untranslatability, which is but an old chestnut. When we speak of a concrete poem, or other aesthetically-inclined composition, as untranslatable, what assumptions are we making about the nature of translation? Do we think of untranslatability as an inherent textual attribute of concrete poetry or as an emergent construct issuing from a particular, normative conception of translation? In relation to Chen Li's concrete poetry, we have witnessed how untranslatability tends to become a convenient recourse to justify why one should *not* translate. Underlying this stance is a fetishization of linguistic or cultural specificity, which has implications for how we approach experimental writing in translation.

The fetish for the untranslatable accrues from a long-standing but not-yet-obsolete tendency in the field to emphasize the *discontents* of translation, namely what translation cannot do or aspire to achieve. This penchant for difference can be traced to an interest in linguistic and cultural incommensurability, perhaps originating in early prescriptive studies whose contrastive-linguistic focus aims exclusively at managing structural differences between any two languages. Such an enterprise in linguistic matching can never be entirely satisfactory, of course, and the irreconcilabilities that remain become the intrigues of translation studies, a source of fascination feeding into and in turn driven by abundant case studies. Indeed a certain satisfaction seems to derive from the understanding that translation inevitably fails us, hence exposing the gaps that cannot be filled, the differences that cannot be reconciled. Discontinuities in translation seem eminently more interesting than continuities, leading to an emphasis on that irreducible core of identity differentiating each language and culture.

Difference is, of course, a good thing through and through; how we respond to difference, however, is quite another matter. As far as translation is concerned, we could adopt a defeatist attitude and throw our hands in the air in the name of untranslatability. But we could also leverage translation and its lack thereof to think productively about the dialectics of cultural production. The popularization of the notion of cultural translation, describing how migrants 'introduce an untranslatable foreignness into the realm of the familiar' (Conway 2019: 130), thereby 'dramatiz[ing] the activity of culture's untranslatability' (Bhabha 1994: 321), has enhanced the theoretical purchase of untranslatability within the humanities. Here untranslatability becomes a crucible for the theorization of hybridity as a fundamental cultural condition in an age of global migrations.

Going further down the road is Barbara Cassin's (2014) ambitious lexicon project *Dictionary of Untranslatables* (*Vocabulaire européen des philosophies: Dictionnaire des intraduisibles*), which highlights 'the principal symptoms of difference in languages' (xvii). What Cassin's *Dictionary* demonstrates is that untranslatability does not suggest absolute opaqueness in meaning and hence non-communicability. On the contrary, the fact that a dictionary can be edited around apparently culture-specific terms in philosophy suggests that, even if translation cannot be realized in economical or 'thin' formations (cf. Appiah's (1993) 'thick translation'), there are alternative modalities in which *the translational* can be manifested, such as comparative etymologies across languages. Inasmuch as *Dictionary* unravels the untranslatable by exposing cross-cultural ambiguities in lexical items, it also abstains from 'a sacralization of the untranslatable, based on the idea of an absolute incommensurability of languages and linked to the near-sanctity of certain languages' (xviii).

Building on the translational ethos of Cassin's work, Emily Apter (2013) argues that untranslatability should be foregrounded in translation history, a history ideally characterized by 'a decided emphasis on when and where translation happens, *and, especially, on how and why it fails*' (29; emphasis added). This spotlighting on the impasse of translation and 'a non-signifying model of communicability' (30) is meant to reverse the powerful assumption that translation as a cross-cultural praxis is 'a good thing *en soi*' under which the Untranslatable (first letter capitalization by Apter) is repressed, 'blind-sided' (27).

The consequence of this oblivion to and stigmatization of untranslatability is a tendency in world literary studies to gloss over incongruities, to 'zoom over the speed bumps of untranslatability in the rush to cover ground' (Apter 2013: 17). Apter's corrective, then, is to resuscitate incommensurability, to build the Untranslatable more formally into the literary heuristic (18) by refocussing on translation failure. For Apter, translation failure is an underrated concept in translation studies that 'invites elaboration alongside other iterations of the non-translatable: 'lost in translation,' the mistranslated, unreliable translation and the *contresens*, an impassive condition that would seem to nest in language; sometimes discernible as a pull away from language norming' (Apter 2013: 29).

It is with these 'iterations of the non-translatable' that World Literature could deprovincialize its canon, tapping into translation 'to deliver surprising cognitive landscapes hailing from inaccessible linguistic folds' (Apter 2013: 16).[25]

The ludic approach to translation advocated in this study is grounded in a similar view of translation failure, although of interest here is the poetics rather than politics of untranslatability. Whereas straight translation terminates in untranslatability, ludic translation begins with the untranslatable, which compels non-linear, rhizomatic solutions to apparently intractable problems such as those presented by concrete poetry. Prima facie untranslatability presents a window of opportunity for ludic translators to experiment with performative renditions. Untranslatability is not a nemesis; it presents a wager that risk-tolerant translators can choose to take up, so long as they are prepared to be frustrated or to fail.

Rethinking Textuality and Authorship

Ludic translation, as I have shown, is a memetic process by which a literary work moves beyond the linguistic-semiotic perimeters of its embodying text. Through this movement, a work mutates itself from one language into another through a procedure that encompasses but also exceeds translation. This has important implications for the ontology of a literary work, that is, what a work of literature *is*.

From the perspective of memesis, a work can be seen as an abstract potential with any number of possible manifestations. Each of these manifestations draws on a different set of affordances that happen to be available and accessible during a translation event. Hence, a single meme (for instance, a conceptual schema governing the aggregated patterning of a concrete poem) can find reverberations and repercussions in different material formations. This recalls Deleuze and Guattari's (1987) concept of *folding*, through which 'a single abstract Animal', or topological animal, 'can be folded and stretched

---

[25] Venuti (2019) is critical of the notion of untranslatability underpinning Cassin's and Apter's work. He argues that Cassin's charge of the mistranslations of medieval French philosophical terms is 'an anachronistic move' that imposes 'a bête noire of contemporary French philosophy' (58) on medieval texts, hence reducing interpretive possibilities to verbal error via a latent instrumentalism governing Cassin's dictionary. Venuti further charges that Apter's conception of untranslatability is 'essentialist': 'Chapter after chapter [in *Against World Literature*] shows that Apter's exposition intensifies the questionable effects of the instrumentalism she inherits from Cassin's dictionary' (66). Venuti takes Apter to task for her definition of the untranslatable as 'an incorruptible or intransigent nub of meaning that triggers endless translating in response to its singularity' (Apter 2013: 235). For Venuti, the very idea of an 'incorruptible or intransigent nub of meaning' betrays Apter's 'semantic essentialism leading to judgments of mistranslations that favour her own interpretation' (Venuti 2019: 66). In the terms I develop here, what Apter calls 'an incorruptible or intransigent nub of meaning' points to the meme of a literary work, which can be variably interpreted and subject to 'endless translating in response to its singularity'.

into the multitude of different animal species that populate the world'
(DeLanda 2016: 151):

> A unique plane of consistency or composition for the cephalopod and the
> vertebrate; for the vertebrate to become an octopus or Cuttlefish, all it would
> have to do is fold itself in two fast enough to fuse the elements of the halves
> of its back together, then bring its pelvis up to the nape of its neck and gather
> its limbs together, into one of its extremities.
>
> (Deleuze and Guattari 1987: 255)

On this view, a literary work is a topographical form with the potential to spin
off into different manifestations as virtual options. For DeLanda (2016: 130),
that topographical form is the *diagram*, which 'captures the structure of the
space of possibilities associated with an assemblage's variable components'.
Žižek (2018: 20) cites an example directly relevant to translation: the transposition of Shakespeare's plays into contemporary settings with 'a different twist
without losing their effectiveness' demonstrates the workings of a literary
assemblage whose elements are relatively autonomous and therefore subject
to 'radical recontextualization'.

Non-human agents play a role in this process too. With reference to the
transposition of print texts to electronic environments, Hayles (2005) proposes
the concept of work-as-assemblage as a heuristic for understanding how a work
disperses its textuality across different material platforms to create what I would
call *distributed texts*. Work-as-assemblage designates 'a cluster of related texts
that quote, comment upon, amplify, and remediate one another' (Hayles 2005:
105); it is the textual counterpart of Deleuze and Guattari's rhizomatic construct, Body without Organs.

Hayles's (2005) argument is that electronic texts differ from print texts in
terms of their materiality, defined as the interaction of the embodied characteristics of a text with its signifying strategies (277). Therefore, the intermediation of a print text on an electronic platform (e.g., the digitization of William
Blake's oeuvre into an electronic and interactive archive) would give rise to
a different text if substantive differences in materiality can be found, that is, if
the electronic version of the work is inflected by the affordances of the
technological media. Equally, the same phenomenon can be theorized in
terms of how the same resources, or memes, tend to be circulated across
different media, leading to what Henry Jenkins (2006) calls 'media convergence'. Hence, as a work distributes itself, the embodying media (construed
broadly to encompass the linguistic medium) converge within the assemblage,
such that a work becomes overdetermined in being worked through any
number of times in different languages, modes, and media.

On this account, a Shakespeare play may be seen as an enfoldable template generating infinite cycles of translations and adaptations. These include YouTube re-mediations around Shakespeare, whose writing serves as 'an available template repeated across YouTube', acquiring 'meme-like properties' (S. O'Neill 2014: 44). The Bard's oeuvre, through multiple re-mediations on YouTube, is turned into 'a network of connections between disparate digital objects" (16). These digital objects, including vernacular film productions, fan-made videos, classroom-based performances, online Shakespearean quote generators, and Shakespeare-related mobile apps, embody various memeings of Shakespeare, through which 'we can see how Shakespeare's meaning is invariably filtered through and contingent on the present, on the specificities of a time, place and their cultural dominants' (47). We can thus speak of a global Shakespeare not just in terms of the translation and circulation of his plays in the world's languages but also in terms of a transmedial poetics derived from their memesis.

Applying this to the case at hand, each of Chen Li's concrete poems discussed earlier is analogous to Deleuze and Guattari's 'abstract Animal'. We can speak of each poem as a semiotic assemblage whose components are capable of being deterritorialized from its original constellation and reterritorialized into different linguistic-semiotic formations, each existing as a virtual option in the 'diagram' of the Chinese original and giving it their own twist. What my ludic translations have done is to enfold Chen Li's Chinese poems across languages, modes, and media, and in that process discover 'in the source text lines, developments of ideas, which hitherto had remained invisible, which might not have been released but for the unforeseen insinuations of new dispositional demands' (Scott 2020: 79). Here, a series of questions provoked by Clive Scott becomes relevant:

> What is it to author a poem, as opposed to authoring what the poem itself seems to make possible? What if the poem is the total poem, that is, the totality of its possible variants and variations, formal and textual, rather than the apparently 'original' text? (Scott 2020: 79)

A possible response is that my iterations of Chen Li's poems converge into a work-as-assemblage (à la Hayles), a text-complex that may have originated with a singular text by the poet but does not reside entirely in that text or even with the poet himself. Rather, the ownership of such a text-complex is shared between the poet and his translator(s). In translating 'Nation', 'Pyramid in Flames', and 'Insects for Breakfast', for instance, I worked in close consultation with Chen Li, enquiring about his motivations behind certain details of textual design (he was always happy to supply more information than

I needed), while making sure to maintain my autonomy in the course of conceiving the translations.

Hence, although my transcreations radically deviate from Chen Li's poems in form, the poet is always kept in the loop throughout the translating process. In a sense, my ludic translations extend the experimental ethos that undergirds the aesthetic of Chen Li's concrete poetry. So where does this locate Chen Li within my ludic translation scheme? Let us recall at this point what Clive Scott says about the imperative to

> distinguish between a translation which purports, in some form or another, to be 'Baudelaire', and translations which seek, thanks to the continuing activity of the ST, either to co-author with Baudelaire (dialogue/communion), or to produce a not-Baudelaire, where Baudelaire is still present in the 'notness'.
>
> (Scott 2012: 3)

By the same token, my ludic elaborations of Chen Li's poems cannot purport to be 'Chen Li'. Rather, they are a collaborative effort between the poet and myself. Because the resulting translations are dramatically different in outlook, they are paradoxically *not-Chen Li* even as we recognize that Chen Li 'is still present in the "notness"' of my transcreations. It is in this sense that we might speak of the *distribution* of a literary work across its translational manifestations and, along with that, a *distributed authorship*. This line of thinking opens up the virtual space for a translation to add value to the source text, even to outstrip the original by reworking its memes in a way that exceeds it far beyond the author's anticipation. My transcreations of Chen Li's work can thus be said to extend, enfold, and distribute each of his texts into a work-as-assemblage, which includes the original Chinese, my translation, and other potential renditions yet to come.

On a more philosophical level, the potential of a work to enfold itself centrifugally is always already there. Yet this potentiality need not be imagined as a pure In-itself, as some essence locked into the linguistic sign. Žižek (2018: 34) uses an interesting analogy to make the point that 'what an object is in itself . . . is not immanent to it independently of its relations to others':

> In the same way, in eroticism, new 'potentialities' of sexual pleasure are what a good lover brings out in you: s/he sees them in you even though you were unaware of them. They are not a pure In-itself, which was already there before it was discovered; they are an In-itself that is generated through a relationship with the other (lover). (Žižek 2018: 33)

Analogously, the potentiality of a literary work to unravel outward is not so much immanent as it is relational. It arises through the interaction of the work's memes with the affordances of languages, modes, and media as well as the distribution of those memes into other semiotic frameworks. And it is through such interaction and distribution that this potentiality becomes instantiated in concrete forms that enter into an intertextual-substrate relation with the originating text. This is where the notion of chance and risk enter the game. Following Žižek (2018), the potentiality of Chen Li's concrete poetry is not an In-itself. As my textual analysis in the previous section has shown, the unravelling of memes may be facilitated or blocked, contingent as it is on a host of factors beyond the text, such as my subjective knowledge base, imaginative proclivities, and technical know-how. It is these and other unforeseeable factors that bring forth or, as the case may be, suppress a poem's memes, resulting in differential outcomes in translation. A literary text *in-translation*, therefore, is always one *in-transition*.

Redesigning Pedagogies

It is not difficult to conceive of ludification as an underlying model for new pedagogies to promote the idea of play in translation and the creative arts in general. This means repackaging a translation task in a problem-and-solution format and facilitating it as an intersemiotic game where students are asked to resolve a given textual issue in groups and in competition with one another. A typical challenge would involve having students transcreate a discursive text using the interlingual, multimodal, and transmedial resources at their disposal. For example, students could be asked to adapt the imagery of a classical Japanese haiku into an English fable, recast it in a contemporary urban setting, and perform it in the style of virtual story-telling using such digital tools as Adobe Slate and ACMI Generator. Or they could be asked to doodle on a piece of paper their cognitive-perceptual responses to a poem read aloud or a sequence of sounds being played. Students would be encouraged to talk about their transcreations freely without a priori valuations about rightness or wrongness. Students might then be asked to vote on each other's ludic translations based on both the aesthetic output and the metalinguistic talk.

The AHRC-funded network Experiential Translation offered a series of workshops that exemplified this kind of gamic pedagogy.[26] For example, 'Soundscapes – Translating from Music' was a short course conducted on Zoom (8 April–6 May 2022) designed to provide 'an introduction to the meaning-making potential of music, with a view to ultimately stimulating

---

[26] The quotations in this paragraph are taken from the website https://experientialtranslation.net /events/.

the production of intersemiotic translations into other media, such as draw-ing, poetry, mime or dance'. Its activities were designed 'to heighten aware-ness of the semiotic potential inherent in the Western musical tradition through a series of listening exercises and discussions, before mobilizing this knowledge in the production of a new creative work'. Another example is the two-part workshop, 'Drawing, Asemic Writing and the Temptation of Translation', which engaged participants 'in a series of drawing exercises and activities designed to question mark-making in response to things unseen, such as time and space occupied by sounds and place'. Participants would then exchange their asemic writings (writings without alphabets) with each other 'to read them, to decipher their rhythm, their mood, their material presence, the effect it produces on the reader/viewer' – in other words, to translate writings *without words*.

Gamic pedagogies such as these afford teachers and students a parallel experience in translation that focuses on experimental rather than instrumental texts. But all pedagogy must lead to some expected outcome. The question then arises as to what kind of rubric is needed for assessing the translation of aesthetic texts that both contrasts with and complements the usual rubric for assessing translation in general. In other words, what would a rubric for ludic translation look like?

A convenient point of reference would be the standard criteria for translation in an accreditation environment. Let us take for example the assessment rubrics of NAATI (National Accreditation Authority of Translators and Interpreters), the official translation certification agency in Australia. The Band 1 criteria for NAATI's Certified Translator test comprise the following for the translation of non-specialized texts:[27]

Meaning transfer skill
Translates the propositional content and intent of the message accurately, with no unjustified omissions, insertions and distortions. Demonstrates ability to skilfully resolve all translation problems.

Follow translation brief
Comprehensively follows the specifications provided in the translation brief. Produces a text which takes into account the purpose of the target text, a specified audience and type of communication.

Application of textual norms and conventions
Displays accomplished use of register, style and text structure appropriate to the genre and consistent with the norms and conventions of the target language.

---

[27] www.naati.com.au/wp-content/uploads/2020/10/Certified-Translator-Assessment-Rubrics.pdf

Language proficiency enabling meaning transfer
Consistently uses written language competently and idiomatically, in accordance with the norms of the target language. Demonstrates accomplished use
of lexicon, grammar and syntax, including orthography, punctuation and
terminology.

The rubrics for ludic translation could appropriate this general frame while
postulating diametrically opposite requirements. Based on the parameters set
out earlier, such criteria would substitute transcreation of memes for transfer of
meaning; allow practitioners to create their own translation brief; focus on the
creative deployment of semiotic resources rather than the consistent application
of textual norms; and seek out multimodal literacy rather than language proficiency. A set of hypothetical rubrics might read as follows:

Transcreation skill
Identifies and transcreates the memes of the text, complete with the
necessary omissions, insertions, and distortions to render an aesthetically
viable translation. Demonstrates ability to skilfully resolve all translation
problems by means other than the transfer of propositional content.

Create translation brief
Devises a translation brief with specifications based on the purpose of the
target text, the identity of the target audience, and the type of communication
as stipulated by the translator in collaboration with a real or imagined
commissioner.

Application of semiotic resources
Displays creative use of culturally produced semiotic resources, both
linguistic and non-linguistic, to improvise apt forms in the target context
in transcreating the source text.

Multimodal literacy enabling transcreation
Competently uses target language resources in a creative, performative
manner. Demonstrates accomplished use of multimodal platforms,
including but not limited to digital platforms.

The ludification of translation is not meant to wholly substitute rational-scientific
models of translating. It aims to supplement instrumentalist thinking to
enrich the fabric of our cultural discourses by tapping into our full resource
repertoire across diverse languages, modes, and media. In theory and in
practice, ludic translation is the counterpoint of instrumental translation;
each has its own domain of application. Ludification is especially pertinent
to aesthetic-related discourses, mediating the interface between translation,
creative writing, and multimodal art. In this regard, ludic translation aligns
with current developments that extend the reach of translation toward

contemporary art, that question 'the dominant paradigm of reading in favor of the analysis of the visual and non-verbal gaps between words, to translate "the reading" into "the looking"' (Vidal 2022: 89). It prompts us to break with the linearity of translation, with its attendant emphasis on what is lost in translation, and to seriously consider the gains of translating playfully.

References

Aarseth, E. 1997. *Cybertext: Perspectives on Ergodic Literature*. Baltimore, MD: Johns Hopkins University Press.

Aarseth, E. 2017. Just games. *Game Studies* 17(1). http://gamestudies.org/1701/articles/justgames

Appiah, A. A. 1993. Thick translation. *Callaloo* 16(4): 808–19.

Apter, E. 2013. *Against World Literature: On the Politics of Untranslatability*. London: Verso.

Baker, M. 2018. *In Other Words: A Coursebook on Translation*. Third edition. Abingdon: Routledge.

Baker, M. 2020. Translation and solidarity in the century with no future: prefiguration vs. aspirational translation. *Palgrave Communications* 6. https://doi.org/10.1057/s41599-020-0400-0

Bassnett, S., ed. 2019. *Translation and World Literature*. Abingdon: Routledge.

Bassnett, S. 2020. Concrete poetry, playfulness and translation. In J. Corbett and T. Huang, eds., *The Translation and Transmission of Concrete Poetry*. Abingdon: Routledge, pp. 9–20.

Bassnett, S. and Bush, P., eds. 2007. *The Translator as Writer*. London: Continuum.

Baynham, M. and Lee, T. K. 2019. *Translation and Translanguaging*. Abingdon: Routledge.

Bhabha, H. 1994. *The Location of Culture*. London: Routledge.

Boase-Beier, J., Fisher, L., and Furukawa, H., eds. 2018. *The Palgrave Handbook of Literary Translation*. London: Palgrave.

Bolter, J. D. and Grusin, R. 1999. *Remediation: Understanding New Media*. Cambridge, MA: MIT Press.

Bruno, C. 2012. Words by the look: issues in translating Chinese visual poetry. In J. St André and H. Peng, eds., *China and Its Others: Knowledge Transfer through Translation, 1829–2010*. Amsterdam: Rodopi, pp. 245–76.

Campbell, M. and Vidal, R., eds. 2019. *Translating across Sensory and Linguistic Borders: Intersemiotic Journeys between Media*. London: Palgrave.

Cassin, B., ed. 2014. Introduction. In B. Cassin, E. Apter, J. Lezra, and M. Wood, eds., *Dictionary of Untranslatables: A Philosophical Lexicon*. Princeton, NJ: Princeton University Press, pp. xvii–xx.

Chan, T. H. 2020. *Western Theory in East Asian Contexts: Translation and Transtextual Rewriting*. London: Bloomsbury.

Chang, F.- l. 2014. Translator's introduction. In C. Li, *The Edge of the Island: Poems of Chen Li*. Trans. Chang F.-l. Taipei: Bookman, pp. 11–23.

Chen L. (2014). *The Edge of the Island: Poems of Chen Li*. Trans. Chang F.-l. Taipei: Bookman.

Chen, L. (2020). Writing and translating concrete poetry in Chinese characters. In J. Corbett and T. Huang, eds., *The Translation and Transmission of Concrete Poetry*. Abingdon: Routledge, pp. 56–70.

Chiu, K.- f. 2018. 'Worlding' world literature from the literary periphery: four Taiwanese models. *Modern Chinese Literature and Culture* 30(1): 13–41.

Conway, K. 2019. Cultural translation. In M. Baker and G. Saldanha, eds., *Routledge Encyclopedia of Translation Studies*, Abingdon: Routledge, pp. 129–33.

Corbett, J. 2020. Introduction. In J. Corbett and T. Huang, eds., *The Translation and Transmission of Concrete Poetry*. Abingdon: Routledge, pp. 1–8.

Cowley, S. 2021. Reading: skilled linguistic action. *Language Sciences* 84. https://doi.org/10.1016/j.langsci.2021.101364

Dawkins, R. 2006. *The Selfish Gene*. 30th anniversary edition. New York: Oxford University Press.

DeLanda, M. 2016. *Assemblage Theory*. Edinburgh: Edinburgh University Press.

Deleuze, G. and Guattari, F. 1987. *A Thousand Plateaus: Capitalism and Schizophrenia*. Trans. B. Massumi. Minneapolis, MN: University of Minnesota Press.

Deterding, S. 2012. Gamification: designing for motivation. *Interactions* 19(4): 14–17.

Deterding, S., Dixon, D., Khaled, R., and Nacke, L. 2011. From game design elements to gamefulness: defining gamification. In *Proceedings of the 15th International Academic MindTrek Conference: Envisioning Future Media Environments*. New York: ACM, pp. 9–15.

Eagleton, T. 2019. *Humour*. New Haven, CT: Yale University Press.

Ensslin, A. 2014. *Literary Gaming*. Cambridge, MA: MIT Press.

Frissen, V., Lammes, S., de Lange, M., de Mul, J., and Raessens, J., eds. 2015. Homo ludens 2.0: play, media, and identity. In V. Frissen, S. Lammes, M. de Lange, J. de Mul, and J. Raessens, eds., *Playful Identities: The Ludification of Digital Media Cultures*. Amsterdam: Amsterdam University Press, pp. 9–50.

Genette, G. 1997[1982]. *Palimpsests: Literature in the Second Degree*. Trans. C. Newman and C. Doubinsky. Lincoln, IN: University of Nebraska Press.

Hayles, K. 2005. *My Mother Was a Computer: Digital Subjects and Literary Texts*. Chicago, IL: University of Chicago Press.

Hayles, K. 2006. Revealing and transforming: how literature revalues computational practice. *Performance Research* 11(4): 5–16.

Ho, G. 2004. Translating advertisements across heterogeneous cultures. *The Translator* 10(2): 221–43.

Huizinga, J. 1955[1938]. *Homo Ludens: A Study of the Play-Element in Culture*. Boston, MA: The Beacon Press.

Huotari, K. and Hamari, J. 2017. A definition for gamification: anchoring gamification in the service marketing literature. *Electron Markets* 27: 21–31.

Hutcheon, L. 2013. *A Theory of Adaptation*. Abingdon: Routledge.

Jackson, K. D. 2020. Transcreation without borders. In J. Corbett and T. Huang, eds., *The Translation and Transmission of Concrete Poetry*. Abingdon: Routledge, pp. 97–111.

Jenkins, H. 2006. *Convergence Culture: Where Old and New Media Collide*. New York: New York University Press.

Kress, G. and van Leeuwen, T. 2021. *Reading Images: The Grammar of Visual Design*. Third edition. Abingdon: Routledge.

Larsen, L. J. 2019. Play and gameful movies: the ludification of modern cinema. *Games and Culture* 14(5): 455–77.

Lecercle, J.-J. 1990. *The Violence of Language*. London: Routledge.

Lee, J. W. 2022. Translanguaging research methodologies. *Research Methods in Applied Linguistics*.

Lee, T. K. 2017. The Chinese cybertext. *Modern Chinese Literature and Culture* 29(1): 173–203.

Lewis, P. E. 1985. The measure of translation effects. In J. Graham, ed., *Difference in Translation*. Ithaca, NY: Cornell University Press, pp. 31–62.

Li, W. 2016. New Chinglish and the post-multilingualism challenge: translanguaging ELF in China. *Journal of English as a Lingua Franca* 5(1): 1–25.

Malmkjær, K. 1987. Translating concrete poetry. *Ilha do Desterro* 17: 33–46.

Malmkjær, K. 2020. *Translation and Creativity*. Abingdon: Routledge.

McGann, J. 1990. How to read a book. In D. Oliphant and R. Bradford, eds., *New Directions in Textual Studies*. Austin, TX: Harry Ransom Humanities Research Center and the University of Texas, pp. 13–37.

Montfort, N. 2001. Cybertext killed the hypertext star. *electronic book review*. www.altx.com/ebr/ebr11/11mon/index.html

Nida, E. 1964. *Towards a Science of Translating, with Special Reference to Principles and Procedures Involved in Bible Translating*. Leiden: Brill.

Nord, C. 2018. *Translating as a Purposeful Activity: Functionalist Approaches Explained*. Second edition. Abingdon: Routledge.

O'Neill, P. 2014. *Transforming Kafka: Translation Effects*. Toronto: University of Toronto Press.

O'Neill, S. 2014. *Shakespeare and YouTube: New Media Forms of the Bard.* London: Bloomsbury.

Perteghella, M. and Loffredo, E., eds. 2006. *Translation and Creativity: Perspectives on Creative Writing and Translation Studies.* London: Continuum.

Raessens, J. 2006. Playful identities, or the ludification of culture. *Games and Culture* 1(1): 52–7.

Raessens, J. 2014. The ludification of culture. In M. Fuchs, S. Fizek, P. Ruffino, and N. Schrape, eds., *Rethinking Gamification.* Lüneburg: Meson Press, pp. 91–114.

Rafael, V. L. 2016. *Motherless Tongues: The Insurgency of Language amid Wars of Translation.* Durham, NC: Duke University Press.

Raley, R. 2016. Algorithmic translations. *CR: The New Centennial Review* 16(1): 115–37.

Salovaara, P. and Statler, M. 2019. Always already playing: hermeneutics and the gamification of existence. *Journal of Management Inquiry* 28(2): 149–52.

Sanders, J. 2016. *Adaptation and Appropriation.* Second edition. Abingdon: Routledge.

Scott, C. 2011a. From the intermedial to the synaesthetic: literary translation as centrifugal practice. *Comparative Critical Studies* 8(1): 39–59.

Scott, C. 2011b. The translation of reading: a phenomenological approach. *Translation Studies* 4(2): 213–29.

Scott, C. 2012. *Literary Translation and the Rediscovery of Reading.* Cambridge: Cambridge University Press.

Scott, C. 2018. *The Work of Translation.* Cambridge: Cambridge University Press.

Scott, C. 2019. Synaesthesia and intersemiosis: competing principles in literary translation. In M. Campbell and R. Vidal, eds., *Translating across Sensory and Linguistic Borders: Intersemiotic Journeys between Media.* London: Palgrave, pp. 87–111.

Scott, C. 2020. Apollinaire's octosyllabic quatrain, translation and zoopoetics. In S. Kay and T. Mathews, eds., *The Modernist Bestiary: Translating Animals and the Arts through Guillaume Apollinaire, Raoul Dufy and Graham Sutherland.* London: UCL Press, pp. 74–91.

Shen, C.-S. and Wu, Y.-P. 2012. Translating beyond languages: the challenges of rendering Taiwan's visual concrete poems in English. *The AALITRA Review* 5: 15–30.

Solon, O. 2013. Richard Dawkins on the Internet's hijacking of the word 'meme'. *Wired* (20 June). https://web.archive.org/web/20130709152558if_/

http://www.wired.co.uk/news/archive/2013-06/20/richard-dawkins-memes/viewgallery/305430

Tymoczko, M. 2014. *Enlarging Translation, Empowering Translators*. Abingdon: Routledge.

Van Leeuwen, T. 2022. *Multimodality and Identity*. Abingdon: Routledge.

Varis, P. and Blommaert, J. 2015. Conviviality and collectives on social media: virality, memes, and new social structures. *Multilingual Margins* 2(1): 31–45.

Venuti, L. 2003. Translating Derrida on translation: relevance and disciplinary resistance. *The Yale Journal of Criticism* 16(2): 237–62.

Venuti, L. 2013. *Translation Changes Everything*. Abingdon: Routledge.

Venuti, L. 2019. *Contra Instrumentalism: A Translation Polemic*. Lincoln, NE: University of Nebraska Press.

Vidal, A. 2022. *Translating Outwards with Contemporary Art*. Abingdon: Routledge.

Vidal, R. and Carter, H. 2021. Some speculations on asemic writing and the productive embrace of uncertainty. https://experientialtranslation.net/2021/07/28/asemic-writing/

Žižek, S. 2018. Marx reads object-oriented ontology. In S. Žižek, F. Ruda and A. Hamza, *Reading Marx*. London: Polity, pp. 17–61.

Acknowledgements

This work would not have been possible without the contribution of my two co-translators, Steven W. K. Chan, who contributed to my design of 'Aurora', 'Solar', 'Sunyata', 'Pyramid in Flames', and 'Insects for Breakfast', and Huang Tao, who assisted me in conceiving 'Nation' and 'Insects for Breakfast'. Max Lee helped me typeset 'Light' several times to produce the visual effect I wanted, for which I am grateful.

Special thanks are due to the poet Chen Li for giving me privileged insight into his world of concrete poetry; to Clive Scott for granting me permission to reproduce his translation of 'Bohémiens en voyage' and for his wonderful experimentations with literary translation that have proved inspiring; to Stephen Cowley for sharing his theoretical ideas on reading as skilled linguistic action; to Kirsten Malmkjær for her interest in and support for the project; and to my anonymous reviewers for their useful suggestions.

I would also like to acknowledge the AHRC-funded network Experiential Translation (https://experientialtranslation.net/), whose exciting initiatives around intersemiotic translation have been a wonderful resource for my work on concrete poetry.

Lastly, this open-access publication is supported by the Louis Cha Fund for East West Studies, administered through the Arts Faculty of the University of Hong Kong.

Cambridge Elements $\equiv$

Translation and Interpreting

Kirsten Malmkjær
University of Leicester

Kirsten Malmkjær is Professor Emeritus of Translation Studies at the University of Leicester. She has taught Translation Studies at the universities of Birmingham, Cambridge, Middlesex and Leicester and has written extensively on aspects of both the theory and practice of the discipline. *Translation and Creativity* (London: Routledge) was published in 2020 and *The Cambridge Handbook of Translation*, which she edited, was published in 2022. She is preparing a volume entitled *Introducing Translation* for the Cambridge Introductions to Language and Linguistics series.

Sabine Braun
University of Surrey

Sabine Braun is Professor of Translation Studies and Director of the Centre for Translation Studies at the University of Surrey. She is a world-leading expert on interpreting and on research into human and machine interaction in translation and interpreting, and holds an Expanding Excellence in England grant to investigate technology-assisted methods, modalities and socio-technological practices of translation and interpreting. She has written extensively on the theory and practice of interpreting, including *Videoconference and remote interpreting in criminal proceedings*, with J. Taylor, 2012; *Here or there: Research on interpreting via video link*, with J. Napier and R. Skinner, 2018. She is editing *Innovation in audio description research*, with K. Starr (2019), and guest-editing a special issue of the *Interpreter and Translator Trainer* with Russo (2020). She is a member of the AHRC Peer Review College.

Editorial Board

About the Series
Elements in Translation and Interpreting present cutting edge studies on the theory, practice and pedagogy of translation and interpreting. The series also features work on machine learning and AI, and human-machine interaction, exploring how they relate to multilingual societies with varying communication and accessibility needs, as well as text-focused research.

Elements in the Series

Printed in the United States
by Baker & Taylor Publisher Services